Witnesses for Change

Witnesses for Change

Quaker Women
over Three Centuries

Edited by
ELISABETH POTTS BROWN
and
SUSAN MOSHER STUARD

Rutgers University Press
New Brunswick and London

Library of Congress
Cataloging-in-Publication Data

Witnesses for change : Quaker women over three
centuries / edited by Elisabeth Potts Brown and
Susan Mosher Stuard.
p.   cm.
Bibliography: p.
Includes index.
ISBN 0-8135-1447-9 (cloth)   ISBN 0-8135-1448-7 (pbk.)
1. Women, Quaker.   I. Brown, Elisabeth Potts, 1939–
II. Stuard, Susan Mosher.
BX7748.W64W58   1989
289.6′088042—dc 19   88-27157

British Cataloging-in-Publication
information available

Contents

v

Contents

vi

Preface

THIS VOLUME, the collected papers of a conference entitled "Witnesses for Change: Quaker Women 1650–1987" held at Haverford College 6 April 1987, makes extraordinary claims for the contribution of Quaker women since the middle years of the seventeenth century. These transcend mere claims that great women like Margaret Fell or Susan B. Anthony arose out of the Quaker tradition. The volume finds a general and widespread greatness among Quaker women over the centuries.

The story begins among a small band of believers in England in the seventeenth century, then crosses the Atlantic to include the American colonial experience in the subsequent century. In the nineteenth century the story moves well beyond the Society of Friends to examine Quaker women's leading roles in gaining abolition, suffrage, and political reform. In the twentieth century, Quaker women's witness for peace has widened into a global program. In each essay Quaker women are placed in the larger context of an increasingly complex modern society where women generally faced greater restrictions on their lives, sometimes at the very moment when Quaker women were expanding theirs. The authors examine how women in the Society of Friends perceived and responded to a religious tradition where the primary demand upon the believer is that she or he live according to privately held values (implying, of course, that each take care to formulate those values). The dilemmas Quaker women have faced at each stage of this remarkable history receive attention.

Following each essay we have included an exhibit from Quaker women's writings beginning with seventeenth-century tracts and letters and continuing with diaries, minutes of Quaker meetings, letters, and reports. These documents create their own dialogue among Quaker women over the centuries and allow the reader to make direct contact with the women of earlier generations who, following their own professed convictions, embarked upon courses that have meant momentous change for society. The last essay acquaints us with the priceless documents that Quaker women have left us, permitting us to learn about their history. The volume taken as a whole asks us to ponder how, and why, a small, close band of women discovered the means to transform their society and break open new paths for others to follow.

We would like to thank Harry Payne (then provost at Haverford College, now president of Hamilton College) for his support for the conference on Quaker women, "Witnesses for Change," where the ideas in this volume were first presented. J. William Frost, Jenkins Professor of Quaker History and Research and director of the Friends Historical Library at Swarthmore College; Edwin B. Bronner, curator of the Quaker Collection and professor of history at Haverford College; and Kenneth L. Carroll, professor of religious studies (retired), Southern Methodist University, generously read essays in the volume. Francis Early, associate professor of history at Mount Saint Vincent University, Halifax, read and commented on an essay as well, for which we thank her. Barbara Curtis, and the entire board of the Friends Historical Association, deserve our thanks for the support and assistance they have given us. Eva Myer of the Quaker Collection, Haverford College, generously typed parts of the manuscript while Diana Alten, Sheila Hallowell, and Jack Eckert, also of the Quaker Collection, gave generous help toward the success of the conference on Quaker women. Carol E. Hoffecker, University of Delaware, Patricia U. Bonomi, New York University, Margaret Hope Bacon, and Mildred Scott Olmsted shared their insights and wisdom with us at the conference. Anna-Liisa Little helped prepare the index. We owe a more general debt of gratitude to the students of Quaker and women's history, as well as concerned Quaker women who attended the Haverford conference in April 1987 and have encouraged us to publish the proceedings.

We wish to thank the Swarthmore College Peace Collection, Women's International League for Peace and Freedom, the Quaker Collection at Haverford College, Friends House Library, London, the University of Rochester, and the University of Chicago Press for permission to reprint the documents that follow each essay.

Contributors

ELISABETH POTTS BROWN has been Quaker bibliographer at Haverford College since 1982. She also serves as secretary for the Friends Historical Association Board and is a member of the Records Committee of Philadelphia Yearly Meeting. She was convener of the 1988 Conference of Quaker Historians and Archivists and recently presented a paper on "East Asian Resources in the Quaker Collection, Haverford College." Brown attended Swarthmore College, received her B.A. from the University of Pennsylvania in 1972 and earned a M.S.L.S. from Drexel University in 1975.

President of Smith College since 1985, MARY MAPLES DUNN is also coauthor of the recently published *The World of William Penn* and *The Founding of Pennsylvania*. She coedited *The Papers of William Penn*, and her articles have appeared in *Notable American Women, Women of America*, and *American Quarterly*. A 1954 Phi Beta Kappa graduate of William and Mary, Dunn received her Ph.D. from Bryn Mawr in 1959.

NANCY A. HEWITT received her B.A. degree from State University of New York at Brockport, where she worked under Susan Stuard, and her Ph.D. at the University of Pennsylvania. Her publications include *Women's Activism and Social Change: Rochester, New York, 1822–1872;* and articles in *Feminist Studies* (1986); and *Social History* (1985). She is currently associate professor of history at the University of South Florida and is researching a book on women, work, and politics in Tampa, Florida.

PHYLLIS MACK is an associate professor of history at Rutgers University, where she joined the faculty in 1972. She has recently served as acting director of the Institute for Research on Women at Rutgers University. Mack was a T. Wistar Brown Fellow at Haverford College's Quaker Collection in 1982–1983. The author of

Calvinist Preaching and Iconoclasm in the Netherlands, 1544–1569,
Mack has published in *Feminist Studies* and *SIGNS,* and has written
a chapter in *Women and the Enlightenment.* A 1961 graduate of Barnard College, Mack received an M.A. from San Francisco State
College in 1966 and a Ph.D. from Cornell University in 1974.

JEAN R. SODERLUND is assistant professor of history at the University of Maryland, Baltimore County. Formerly she was curator of
the Swarthmore College Peace Collection. She is author of *Quakers
and Slavery: A Divided Spirit,* articles on Quaker women, and is
currently working on a project on mid-Atlantic women, religion,
and reform. Soderlund was an assistant editor for *The Papers of
William Penn.* She received her B.A. in 1968 from Douglass College and her Ph.D. in 1982 from Temple University.

After serving as director of the Women's Archives, now the Schlesinger Library, and of the Radcliffe Seminars, BARBARA MILLER
SOLOMON became a Radcliffe and then a Harvard dean. In 1975, as
senior lecturer on History and Literature and on the History of
American Civilization, she pioneered in teaching women's history
to Harvard graduate and undergraduate students. She received her
B.A. in 1940 and Ph.D. in 1953 from Radcliffe and Harvard, respectively. She is the author of *In the Company of Educated Women: A
History of Women and Higher Education in America; Ancestors and
Immigrants: A Changing New England Tradition;* and *Pioneers in Service: the History of the Associated Jewish Philanthropies of Boston.* Her
other publications include four essays in *Notable American Women;*
she is an editor of a 12-volume Garland series "Educated Women:
Higher Education, Culture, and Professionalism, 1850–1950."

SUSAN MOSHER STUARD holds a Ph.D. from Yale University in
medieval economic and social history. She came to the study of
Quakers through women's history and investigation of gender issues. Her interest in women may be seen in twin volumes from
University of Pennsylvania Press, *Women in Medieval Society* and
Women in Medieval History and Historiography. She is currently professor of history at Haverford College.

Introduction

SUSAN MOSHER STUARD

Women's Witnessing: A New Departure

FOR WOMEN the apogee of the Protestant Reformation arrived with Quakerism.[1] In the seventeenth century, Quaker women were preachers and prophets when public expression was denied to any woman outside the royal line. In the eighteenth century, Quaker women consolidated their power in regular women's meetings for business, followed the call to preach abroad, and joined the transforming movement to abolish slavery from human society. In the nineteenth century, Quaker women participated in, and in the most significant cases led, the major reform movements, including that for women's rights and participation in the public sphere. In the twentieth century, Quaker women helped found and remain in the vanguard of the movement for world peace. How can such prodigious claims be made for such a numerically small and often disadvantaged group? The power to transform society is given to few in our modern world and has never been gratuitously offered to Quaker women. Instead, the women set themselves the task of discovering the means of transforming society as their faith directed and, seldom without pain and sacrifice, broke open new paths even when they were unwelcome or directly opposed.

On 6 April 1987 a symposium on Quaker women held at Haverford College presented such findings—and more. It became clear to us then that it was necessary to treat Quaker women's history over its entire span to make their unique contribution to history comprehensible.[2] Therefore, this volume begins with the emergence of the first circle of Friends in seventeenth-century England and brings the story down to the present. The Quaker community has long appreciated the unique heritage of its women, but over the past two decades women's historians have also discovered the exceptional nature of Quaker women's contributions and are seeking to understand it. In turn, feminist history provides us with tools for understanding Quaker women; two approaches favored by feminist scholars appear to be especially pertinent to this investigation. First, these scholars challenge us to multiply the perspectives from which we view history, in order to expand our horizons and gain a fuller understanding of the complex character of women's roles. Next, they provide us one vehicle for doing so: the conscious adoption of a new woman-centered stance from which to view our past.[3]

The investigation of Quaker women's contributions can profit from our adoption of two vantage points particularly: one from outside and one from within the Quaker tradition itself. The first allows us to place Quaker women in the larger context of a society where modernization tended to circumscribe women's lives within ever narrower limits. If, instead, Quaker women enlarged their roles, they did so through successful resistance to societal norms and this is an accomplishment worth study. A double vantage point may also help us to understand the remaining limits on Quaker woman's lives, for not even Quaker women could transcend all the boundaries set out by contemporary Western society. From this viewpoint the remarkable nature of the Quaker accomplishment becomes apparent. The second vantage point, from within the Quaker tradition, may help us understand the reasons why Quaker women transcended the stereotypes of their time and place to play effective, and often transforming, roles in the world. In a religious tradition where the primary demand on the believer is that she or he live according to privately held values, implying, of course, that each person take care to formulate those values, in such a tradition how have women found the will to disregard conventional wisdom about women's subordinate and silent place in society?

Taking the external vantage point into consideration first, the story of Quaker women profits from a long-term perspective; it is best approached by casting the question over an even longer duration than the three centuries since the mid-seventeenth-century birth of the Quaker movement. For one matter seems clear: Quaker women recovered roles in the late Reformation, roles as religious teachers and leaders that had existed earlier but disappeared with the onset of modern times.

England, the birthplace of the Quaker movement, possessed a

long history of significant religious roles for women. The Abbess Hild at Whitby, great-niece of King Edwin of Northumbria, presided over the Synod of 664. She comes down to us in a vivid word portrait by the Venerable Bede.[4] Leader of a great, Christianizing double monastery (inhabited by both men and women), Hild was responsible for the education of England's most important prelates. And Whitby was noted for learning; at least five of its monks trained by Hild were recruited as bishops. Only Hild's prestige could win adherence to the decision reached in 664 to adopt the Roman calendar over the Celtic rite for the celebration of Easter, a decision particularly troubling because Hild gave it her support against her own inclination and interests after prayer and serious questioning. Force of conscience marked Hild's leadership, and the women of the English church who followed her found their own authoritative and persuasive voices through that same means.[5] Women entered holy orders and participated in the great reform movements of the Middle Ages, becoming Cistercians, Gilbertines, and nuns of the Order of Fontevrault. The latter two reform movements placed women in positions of authority over men in double monasteries. Both these orders drew popular support from the English population, which accepted and valued women as guides toward a higher spiritual calling.

By the thirteenth and fourteenth centuries women had largely turned away from the powerful institutional roles they had played in the church and had begun to express their religiosity in mystical writings. Julian of Norwich, a Beguine who wrote *The Revelations of the Divine*[6] in the fourteenth century, illustrates well this turn toward a more individualistic piety. Remarkably learned for a reclusive mystic, Julian showed theological sophistication in her idea of Christ as mother as a way of expressing the nurturing nature of Divine Love.[7] Her vivid imagery opened her revelations to a popular audience hungry for spiritual counseling. The irony of Julian's life stems from her own clear choice to be a reclusive, that is, retired from the world, while a clamorous public sought her guidance and help. Her writings satisfied that public, but we know little else about her. The mystics among medieval women seldom sought influence but, like Julian, wielded it because the public was convinced of their sanctity and special calling.

Nevertheless, the turn inward toward the mystical life was not entirely a freely chosen path for women with a religious calling. The European society that had felt at ease with women in authoritative roles, even holding power over men in certain instances in the early Middle Ages, had changed by the thirteenth century. Betty Bandel traced this development in her 1955 article, "The English Chroniclers' Attitude toward Women."[8] She noted that authoritative roles for women were recorded as if nothing out of the ordinary before the Norman Conquest; but in the twelfth century, chroniclers increasingly labelled such roles as "manly" and unnatural. By the late Middle Ages, the time of Julian of Norwich, chroniclers suspected that earlier works erred in ascribing such acts to women. They no longer believed that women could wield power in public and, in the case of the twelfth-century Empress Matilda, who fought to place her son Henry II on the English throne, reascribed her recorded acts to her brother out of disbelief. Chroniclers of the fourteenth and fifteenth centuries, then, conveyed much stronger assumptions regarding the constraints on women's roles than those who had written before them.

In fact, the great watershed for medieval women occurred in the twelfth and thirteenth centuries when new claims for the relations between specific gender roles and a more universal gender ideology first appeared.[9] Early medieval people had firm assumptions about gender roles but less positive ideas about why women and men differed in their natures from one another; that is to say, they did not advocate any strong gender ideology. In the age of Christianity's expansion, early medieval people were likely to emphasize the likeness of men and women rather than their differences. The equality of all souls before God, regardless of sex, age, or other distinction, was a powerful theme within early medieval Christianity.

With the revival of learning in the twelfth century classical notions about the nature of woman were reintroduced. For the most part these descended to medieval scholars by way of Christian texts, but the opinions on women antedated Christianity. Polar notions about woman were as old as the School of Pythagoras and they were circulated in the works of Aristotle. The reintroduction of a polarized schema where man is first assigned an attribute and then woman is given the opposite (if man is right, woman is left; if man is good, woman is evil) amounted to a rethinking of the woman question. Since this rethinking involved a categorical imperative—thinking about *woman* rather than *women*—a number of novel gender associations entered European life. And when they did, they did so with the authority of the esteemed ancients attached to them. Scholarly opinion asserted that "female nature" was related in a polar juxtaposition to "man's nature."

Under the force of these classical opinions, presented in the learned Latin of scholarly spiritual discourse, few defenses of women were possible. Women were much more likely to think of themselves in terms of their station in life, or "estate," perceiving their interests as similar to their brothers', husbands', fathers', and sons' rather than in terms of their sex. There were still some however who did turn their thoughts to women as women and defended them; Ian Maclean in a very clever book, *The Renaissance Notion of Woman,* introduces us to some of those thinkers who protested the new gender associations.[10] Spirited women like Christine de Pizan spoke in women's defense; but it is worth noting that she was answered by an overwhelming barrage of scholarly disquisition. Clearly the new European gender system based upon revived classical polarities had triumphed by the late medieval centuries and early decades of the Renaissance.

Polarities were unexamined notions rather than rigorously argued ideas and thus they were shared as commonplaces from scholarly discipline to scholarly discipline: theology, medicine, ethics, the law. Through a process of apposition (to man) and alignment of those attributes, Europeans came to possess an authoritative opinion on woman, that is, a gender ideology. This new gender ideology affected gender roles in significant ways. One would not turn to a woman for spiritual leadership if woman is both left and evil. Authoritative opinion could even override what people knew and understood about women so that traditional popular support for women as spiritual leaders did not necessarily prevail against learned opinion presented in sermons, treatises, and lectures in schools.

Identifying this gender ideology in the Renaissance centuries prompted some of the pioneering twentieth-century studies of women's history and led to questioning of the role played in our history by sex-linked stereotypes. Joan Kelly in her pathbreaking 1976 article, "Did Women Have a Renaissance?" argued:

In sum, a new division between personal and public life made itself felt as the state came to organize Renaissance society, and with that division the modern relation of the sexes made its appearance, . . . Renaissance ideas on love and manners, more classical than medieval, and almost exclusively a male product, expressed this new subordination of women to the interests of husbands and male-dominated kin groups and served to justify the removal of women from an 'unladylike' position of power and erotic independence.[11]

Through the spread of literacy, sustained by the development of the printing press, gender ideology entered daily life in communities throughout Europe. If Renaissance courts and cities saw its effects first, the rest of Europe soon followed. Wherever gender ideology was introduced, through sermons, or through the practice of trained lawyers or the nostrums and advice of trained physicians, it affected women's lives in comparable ways. Notions about woman's nature justified a new division between the public sphere as man's domain and a private sphere to which women were relegated. Gender ideology proved to be as powerful as it was subtle. Few responses proved effective antidotes against the assumption that certain behaviors were "unladylike" or "unnatural" for a woman.

We might think that the Reformation, grounded as it was in the impulses of popular piety, might have had the force to break apart these assumptions. Women flocked to the Protestant churches, bringing with them the power of their spiritual enthusiasm. Highborn women served as patrons of the Protestant cause. Women like the Anabaptist Ursula Jost prophesied in the Rhineland region. Since the time of the Lollards in England and the Hussites in Bohemia, women served in the ranks of those who defied religious authority to join the reforming sectarians. In the case of the Hussites, women served alongside men in the military campaigns against Catholic forces.[12]

At issue here is not only women's religious participation but the sway of entrenched gender assumptions. Did the new Protestant churches reject notions about woman's nature when they examined, and rejected, so many of the scholastic doctrines of the medieval church? Clearly Martin Luther challenged scholastic ideas directly and energetically. Specifically, he did battle with the scholastic argument that woman was "a botched male" in God's creation. He did so not necessarily to defend women but to put an end to a disputation he viewed as valueless. He asserted God made woman as any other creature, "with a care he might have devoted to his most noble work." This defense, however, was only achieved by comparing and contrasting woman to that other essential category: man. Luther, alas, did not escape the mental habit of making polar arguments about women.

In his commentary on Genesis 1:27 he said,

Lest woman should seem to be excluded from all glory of future life, Moses mentions both sexes [in Genesis 1:26–27]; it is evident therefore that woman is a different animal to man, not only having different members, but also being far weaker in intellect [*ingenium*]. But although Eve was a most noble creation, like Adam, as regards to the image of God, that is, in justice, wisdom, and salvation, she was nonetheless a woman. For as the sun is more splendid than the moon (although the moon is also a most splendid body) so also woman, although the most beautiful handiwork of God, does not equal the dignity and glory of the male.[13]

Thus, Luther's very defense of woman is made categorical and employs polar constructs. While Luther could and did reject conscious misogyny in ecclesiastical opinion, he continued to use the polar constructions that shaped gender ideology in the Renaissance and Reformation centuries. In doing so he perpetuated an inherited gender system within the dissenting Protestant movement. E. William Monter may then justly question whether women had a reformation since gender ideology was not modified or discarded.[14] It was not enough to reject specific scholastic arguments; the strength of gender ideology could only be overcome by consciously examining and rejecting the polar constructs that shaped those arguments.

John Calvin faced and failed the same challenge. He specifically referred to the medieval theological synthesis as "the labyrinth." In negotiating its pathways in order to formulate Protestant theology in his *Institutes,* Calvin did not discard the assumptions about gender inherent in scholasticism. Rather Calvin was content to see

Protestant women as wives subordinated to their husbands.[15] The challenge presented to reformers and reforming religious groups in the early modern era was daunting if, in truth, they exhibited the desire to rethink intentionally the woman question. Women's roles resisted reform while polar gender ideology remained intact.

This long-term review brings us back to the seventeenth century and the English women who joined the Civil War religious sects. Out of zeal they attempted to recover rather than invent formerly popular roles as spiritual leaders, teachers, and advisors. But just as clearly they made their attempt to do so against powerful entrenched notions about woman's nature that intruded between them and the experience of early medieval holy women. These notions were widely shared across divisions of language, tradition, and religious confession. Much stood between seventeenth-century women and the roles they sought. While tolerable as visionaries and mystics, women had been largely eliminated from positions of power within the church centuries before. The Protestant Reformation of the fifteenth and sixteenth centuries had not challenged and replaced the gender ideology of medieval scholasticism. Furthermore, that set of associations underlay the new wave of witchcraft persecution that swept through England and Scotland in the seventeenth century and even reached the American colonies. As opposite to man, who was understood to be formed in the image of God, woman was understood to be particularly prone to the wiles of the devil. The term "witch" even changed gender: *maleficus* had been a masculine term until the Dominican monks who composed the *Malleus maleficarum* in the fifteenth century recast the term as *malifica*.[16] This handbook for identifying witches assumed that woman, as left and evil, was prone to accept the wiles of the devil, while man, as right and good, was more likely to escape the devil's clutches.

What of the potent mix of religious ferment and political revolt that erupted in England between 1640 and 1680? With women active in the ranks of the Puritan movement and among those more radical Levellers and Ranters who called for the reform of the whole social order, did England's Civil War disturb age-old assumptions about women? Keith Thomas has argued that despite the odds against them women did achieve leadership in the first flush of religious enthusiasm during the era of the Civil War.[17] Yet, he also notes that women tended to be marginalized in the decades that followed when previously rebellious religious groups consolidated their position and developed the rudiments of an institutional church. It was during this stage, when the religious community took on the character of a church, that the traditional gender ideology was brought most fully into play.

Separatist congregations were constantly bombarded by criticism at this stage in their development, that is, immediately after the initial visionary phase of their movement had brought them both converts and notice. Anglican pamphleteers provided powerful ammunition to be turned against separatist congregations with titles like *A Discoverie of six women preachers* (1641).[18] The full force of gender ideology descended on the separatists then when they faced external criticism and sometimes internal dissension for allowing women authoritative roles. It is not at all surprising that such congregations saw the elimination of women from positions as preachers as a small price to pay for a degree of tolerance and respectability and the right to survive. Women's leadership seldom lasted beyond the initial stages in any separatist congregation's formation, although women continued to play important sustaining roles within the group.

Women in the separatist Civil War sects provide an instructive example of just how difficult it was to challenge prevailing assumptions about women's place in a religious movement of the seventeenth century. It was likely to be seen as "unnatural" and surely "unladylike" for women to lead in any public role or capacity. It opened a religious community to attack and censure. It might even court allegations of devil worship and witchcraft. Most insidious of all, gender ideology existed on the conceptual level; it had become conventional wisdom as well as authoritative opinion. Since polar notions of women were mental constructs rather than rigorously argued ideas, they were rarely examined and evaluated, and therefore they were very difficult to dislodge.

This extensive review of women's fortunes through the late medieval, Renaissance, and Reformation centuries serves then to highlight the extraordinary nature of the early Quaker position on women. For Margaret Fell (1614–1702) and George Fox (1624–1691) were not only willing to accord women full equality within the religious community, they asserted that women had every right to testify to God's Word. But is it any surprise that Margaret Fell adopted a defensive tone when she published *Womens speaking justified* in 1666? For a group whose leaders, including Margaret Fell herself, spent long periods in prison, there was surely awareness that women's prominent role was a radical practice and one that laid the community open to censure and persecution. That the Society of Friends maintained their original position on women's ministry becomes then a heroic stand, as heroic as their preaching to the scholars at Cambridge only to be beaten and run out of town or challenging the Restoration monarchy's policies.

In order to understand fully the import of the Quaker movement's departure from tradition on the question of women it is necessary to change vantage points and look at the Quaker movement from within during its earliest years. The Society of Friends looked for the emergence of life and power in the worshipping group, or, in other words, practiced a form of group mysticism similar to the mysticism of the Catholic tradition in its ecstatic and visionary dimension, but distinct in its emphasis upon the group of worshippers rather than the individual. The mystical tradition in which women had long played roles was thus preserved, but also transformed into a collective experience. In contrast to the Protestant church of the Reformation, as Howard Brinton relates, "[Quakers] subtracted all ritual, all programmed arrangement in worship and the professional ministry, allowing for no outward expression except the prophetic voice which had been heard in the New Testament Church in the beginning. They endowed no officials with religious or administrative duties."[19] The elimination of an ecclesiastical hierarchy meant the absence of any institutionalized authority whose agents might enforce a gender ideology within the community. Both early decisions, to forego dogma and a clergy, helped establish a climate of acceptance for women among the Quakers virtually unique in European life in the seventeenth century. Coupled with the affirmation of Margaret Fell as a spiritual leader, a stand confirmed by Fox and other respected men of the community over voiced criticism, Quakerism took a clear stand for women's full and equal participation within the community.

Perhaps this role for women is best understood through comparing Quakers with their Puritan neighbors with whom they shared so much in the way of insights into ethics and worship. As Hugh Barbour has noted, "[Quaker] conflicts with puritan leaders had the loving desperation of a family feud."[20] Thus the Quaker stand that mothers, wives, and daughters may receive, and express, the Word as well as fathers, husbands, and sons, may be understood as a familial quarrel with Puritans about spiritual entitlement. As such it was connected with Friends' profound faith in the primacy of the Spirit that recognizes no man-made distinctions about who receives and relates the Word to others. "Puritan ministers, on the other hand, were by vocation pastors."[21] And pastors were to be men because Puritan women were understood by the men of their families as those who were not called to such public vocations.

Nevertheless a Quaker stand for women and their participation was not sufficient to change definitively the terms of women's participation. Gender ideology, even if it was not enforced by an ecclesiastical hierarchy could not be eliminated by simply ignoring it and hoping it would disappear; it was far too deeply embedded in the culture of seventeenth-century England, and New England for that matter, to cease affecting the attitudes and expectations of the Quakers themselves. Quaker women's religiosity was often at odds with expectations of womanly behavior. Their calling, preaching, and traveling in order to minister forced a rethinking of gender roles for Quaker men who were, in some instances, masters of classical languages and the products of England's best schools. Men faced a clear choice between the Friends' way of the spirit and traditional theological opinions when they came up against the implications of women receiving Divine revelation equally with them.

In the face of this choice the quietist proclivities of George Fox and a few other Quaker men were abandoned and replaced by harsh vocal remonstrance against prevailing scholarly opinions in universities and learned circles. Quakers, both women and men, took positions close to those of the antinomian groups of the seventeenth century and often expressed themselves in words as biting as those of the Ranters. Fox was particularly critical of scholarly argument

13

where form eclipsed spirit. He found the whole dry exercise of scholarly exposition "jangling" and rejected it—not just its fruits but its very exercise—as arid and sterile and against the spirit and the light. Women among the Friends may be credited with helping to arouse righteous indignation against the whole corpus of received scholarly thought and the mental constructs by which thinkers arrived at their conclusions. By rejecting the very endeavor of formulating orthodox doctrines and rules, Quakerism as a movement found a way to discard the gender ideology that lay embedded within Western thought. Viewing the entire inherited canon as spiritually suspect, Barclay, Fox, and others assailed reasoning, syllogisms, mnemonic aids, learned disquisition, and scholarly debate as foul, arid, prideful, and a sure sign of the Fall from Grace wherever it was practiced. From this perspective, Quakers were forced to rethink their entire position on fundamental social and philosophical questions, including their position on the woman question.[22]

George Fox went so far as to state that Paul's scriptural admonition that women be silent in church was no more than a particular chastisement for a particular church where women had yet to be brought to the Light. He wrote *Concerning Sons and Daughters, and Prophetesses speaking and Prophesying in the Law and the Gospel* early in his ministry, making clear the stand he would sustain until his death.[23]

Fox may have done an even greater service for women Quakers through the example of his personal witnessing. Fox reaffirmed the early medieval theme of the likeness of souls before God and employed an imagery of tenderness and sensibility that drew upon attributes assigned to women by early modern times. He took terms associated with women: weak, tender, soft, and applied them to his own mystical soul. His use of language revealed a mind that distinguished gender attributes from sex difference; that is, in his effort to expand the dimensions of his spirit he borrowed freely from both masculine and feminine attributes and just as freely mixed the two in his own accounts of his mystical experiences. Understanding the exercise as spiritually freeing, he effectively challenged the permanent and unyielding nature of gender characteristics.

The liberating nature of a new way of thinking is a story told eloquently by Phyllis Mack in the first essay in this volume. The author puts us in touch with the moving experience through which women found a new path and the determination to follow it. Since Professor Mack speaks so clearly from the internal vantage point of spiritual life within early Quakerism, it may be most useful at this point to move again to a vantage point outside the Quaker community to propel the story onward.

Fortunately, the practices that compose the essential core of Quakerism were formulated within the long lifetime of Margaret Fell. After the death of her first husband and several episodes of imprisonment, Margaret Fell and George Fox married in 1669. Over the next twenty years, and in an atmosphere of persecution until the Act of Toleration of 1689, the guiding hand of Margaret Fell may be found in the established practices of Quakerism. Fox and Fell both advocated a women's business meeting as an opportunity for them to set priorities that might then be shared with the entire Society of Friends.[24] This permitted women to participate in the larger community in the position of advocates for their own acts of charity and ministry. Women extended the voice they had gained as ministers of the spirit with the practical skills learned in their own local meetings.[25]

In the same unobtrusive manner, Margaret Fell and early women supporters of the movement, including Margaret Fell's daughters, settled questions of the religious life such as marriage practices, the care of the sick and poor, and community responsibilities (often, in the early years, responsibilities of care for imprisoned members of the Society) in terms favorable to women's participation and leadership. According to Isabel Ross, the biographer of Margaret Fell, a letter was sent out to Quaker communities everywhere from the Lancashire Meeting between 1675 and 1680.[26] This letter provides instructions for women's meetings, theological justification for women speaking and acting, and a most moving call to battle: "And though wee be looked upon as the weaker vessels, yet strong and powerful is God, whose strength is made perfect in weakness, he can make us good and bold, and valliant Souldiers of Jesus Christ."[27] Quaker women were placed in touch with each other through this widely circulated letter and followed the practice of exchanging visitations and letters through the following decades.

The consequence of this early circulated letter can hardly be overemphasized. Through sharing a common philosophy women's meetings for business on both sides of the Atlantic followed remarkably consistent programs of action. Their remarkableness stems from the fact that this consistency of practice was achieved without structured or bureaucratic form being imposed by authority, that is, by steps that typically accompany the evolution of organizations. Quaker women achieved consistency in their practices through consciously seeking answers about how their sister meetings understood their mission and how they formulated goals for their actions "in the world." They followed a program comparable to that of men's meetings, receiving ministerial visits, sending and receiving letters from other meetings, and trying to live by the ideas set out by George Fox. By the eighteenth century, women might gather at Philadelphia Yearly Meeting to affirm their ties with each other, but this represents the most elaborate stage in their structuring. For the most part, women's meetings managed their own agenda and selected their own priorities. They also kept their own records.[28]

By the mid–eighteenth century, London Quakers did not hold a yearly meeting for women. It is a moot point whether Londoners were affronted by the American Quaker women who arrived in 1753, demanding a yearly meeting for women, more for their presumption or their deportment in the streets (some of them publicly smoked pipes).[29] In time, however, Susanna Morris, an American Quaker who spoke to London Yearly Meeting, demanding women's rights to their own gathering, gained a qualified victory. English women would have their London meeting but that meeting could not make rules binding on the Society at large.

Peripatetic women Friends bound their sisters together in such a web of interlocking ties within that century that oceans and wilderness appear like minor obstacles. The Quaker community of Philadelphia and that of Providence, Rhode Island, were in constant contact through visiting women ministers sent from both sides of the Atlantic Ocean. Women learned from and inspired each other. A ministry of women coming from one meeting was very likely to evoke a ministry returned, knitting together the Caribbean, England, the New England seaports, and the American frontier. Quakerism meant a respite from the isolation that plagued women's lives in the era of new settlement and restless moving on. Women's stated purpose was to take care of one another, their children, and the indigent, then to extend their circle to take care of others who manifested needs, and to heed the call to minister abroad if it were to come to them. The benign effects on the collective mental health of the women themselves need hardly be emphasized. In an age that required heroism to survive, Quaker women found the resources to do more than that: to witness to others and work actively in a myriad of causes.

Likemindedness characterized Quaker women, but Quaker women did not replicate each others' programs. While women might join a cause suggested by other Quakers, such as the abolition of slavery advocated by the witnessing of a traveling minister, Quaker women were free to set their own priorities. Furthermore, they were enjoined to aid a member of their meeting to formulate her witness even if they could not in conscience share it. The strains introduced by such a high standard for mutual support are manifest in Quakerism from an early stage. Likemindedness was never a necessary result of thinking prayerfully together about problems. For this reason Quaker women chose different, sometimes divergent paths. Education consumed the energies of a number of Quaker women who sought education themselves and participated in educating the next generation of women and men. The very success and prosperity of Quaker communities on both sides of the Atlantic Ocean opened opportunities for some women to distribute welfare and initiate reform, or build welfare institutions if they identified the need. It was Conscience that dictated, with the result that Quaker women from the eighteenth century onward were active in most of the reform and progressive movements in Western society. Mary Maples Dunn analyzes their consequential choices in an era of consolidation as members of the Society became highly respected, and often highly successful, members of their various communities. This is a complex story of witnessing and accommodation, of remaining plain or becoming "this world's people."[30]

Quaker worldly success was hardly universal, of course; deep differences were bound to emerge between the wealthy and educated Quakers of the cities and the rural Quakers whose way of life differed little from their seventeenth-century ancestors. By the early years of the nineteenth century Quakers faced choices of divided loyalty focused on reforming leaders and reform movements from within the Society of Friends. New persuasions often delineated economic, social, and political differences. Quaker women were, of course, caught up in the controversies of their community and their choices to follow Joseph John Gurney or Elias Hicks frequently were made in concert with the men in their families; choices among Quakers tended to be family decisions. By and large, historians have rated these religious controversies, which lasted more than a century, injurious to the Quakers as a community and deleterious to the social-action concerns of members of the Society of Friends. Nancy Hewitt challenges this interpretation for Quaker women in nineteenth-century America. She finds that the emphasis upon conscience's dictates brought women to hard choices but that their choices, once made with conviction, empowered women to become pioneers in the movement for reform of women's place in the Western world. Professor Hewitt sees the painful divisions as a crucible for new reform ideas, ideas that might not have emerged had Quaker women remained comfortable in the wholesomeness of their community.

The history of the Quaker movement returns continually to the theme of the consequence of family, friends, and the immediate community in the spiritual growth of the individual.[31] Over the centuries birthright Quaker women may have been raised with an entirely different set of expectations from other women of their day. Yet a Quaker family provided no guarantee that the message of the founders on women's roles would be heeded in the rearing of children. Quaker families have at times reflected all the prejudices against women present in modern society, and they have just as successfully inculcated gender ideology into their daughters and sons, and with the same lack of conscious intent, as their neighbors who were members of confessional churches.

Still, there are many documented cases where Quaker mothers, aunts, and grandmothers inspired daughters. The Coffin family of New England can claim powerful women leaders over generations, including Lucretia Coffin Mott who worked for women's rights. M. Carey Thomas, feminist and president of Bryn Mawr College, came from a formidable line of Quaker women. Quaker communities consistently affirmed the importance of family and in many cases a family served as a nursery for developing personal strength. Mothers exercised spiritual authority rather than the mere domestic control that children could discount as irrelevant to concerns in the greater world.

Fathers could make a crucial difference too, by both what they did and what they failed to do. If they educated and inspired their daughters as well as their sons, and if they failed to expect their daughters to conform to the notions of the day about women's place, they launched powerful daughters into positions of leadership. Susan B. Anthony's Quaker father, Daniel, was a strong influence on his daughter's life-long struggle for the franchise for women. And who can forget the husbands of Quaker women? Abby Kelley Foster's husband Stephen promoted her work and shared her ostracism when her conscience dictated a break with her meeting. So, too, did lesser-known husbands. Isaac Post supported the most radical actions of his wife Amy, such as travelling alongside a black man or wearing bloomers on the public streets. Likewise, Eugene Mosher who married Susan Anthony's younger sister Hannah, marched in demonstrations for women's suffrage. We must remember that these men marching with the feminists were intentionally stoned by onlookers as traitors to their sex; and that it was Quaker men who most often risked themselves by thus supporting women's rights in the nineteenth century.

In some cases, discussion of family leads to a discussion of privilege, for what can be more empowering in modern society than both the means and the desire to educate one's daughters and then support them in their chosen life's work? Five of the first eleven women physicians in America were Quakers. Quaker women also entered other scientific fields that required extensive and expensive educations. Rebecca Pennock Lukens, left a widow at twenty-nine with six children, inherited a steel mill. Thus, both her natal family and a husband who trusted her capacities stood behind her subsequent success as a foremost manufacturer of boilerplate.

We are very clear in this volume that Quaker women have had to overcome serious handicaps, but as Quaker families prospered we may sound an ironic key by noting that occasionally the handicaps for Quaker women were social position, "breeding," wealth, and influence. Mercedes Randall, biographer of the convinced Quaker economist and sociologist Emily Greene Balch, was so exercised about the inference of Balch's great "propriety" and social status that she titled her biography, *Improper Bostonian: Emily Greene Balch.*[32] She perceived that women's privileged backgrounds might actually work against their reform efforts by turning the public against them. On balance, however, Barbara Solomon does not believe Emily Balch suffered from either privilege or particularly on grounds that she was a woman. Her family were enlightened Unitarians, and Emily Balch had the full support of her Quaker colleagues before she joined the Society of Friends in her fifties. She wrote herself that single professional women could take risks for the public good in ways that wives and mothers could not, and her long life brought recognition for her courage and integrity with the award of the Nobel Peace Prize after World War II.

For both Emily Greene Balch and Mildred Scott Olmsted, a Quaker woman who was blessed with education, wealth, and family influence, it was necessary to step out of proscribed roles and family protection to lead the cause for world peace. Barbara Solomon analyzes the choices such women faced in her story of female Friends active in the global peace movement in alliance with other reform-minded women. These women faced a series of dilemmas as they confronted the conflicting demands of pacifist, reform, and feminist agendas that engaged their moral energies.

While privilege played a role in providing education for women and exposing them to global events, the unpopular stands that women took have occasionally excluded them from the advantages of class once they began witnessing for peace. In the era of the Vietnam War that still held true. Quaker women protesting the war sometimes came from well-off backgrounds but that did not protect them from censure as "Commie-lovers" and traitors. In truth, their stake in the American way of life may have actually added to the criticisms lodged against them.

The dilemmas of the twentieth-century reformer cause us to reflect on the social background of Quakers over the past three hundred years. From the very beginning the Quaker community challenged elitism in all its guises, but that did not hinder Quaker families, almost uniquely among the dissenting religious sects of seventeenth-century England, from becoming part of the comfortably-off bourgeoisie in time. Thus, when Quaker women and men have spoken in the name of a cause they spoke as respected persons with a stake in their communities. For instance, a Quaker stand against slavery in a seaport was often a stand against economic self-interest and was understood and respected as such.

It is well to remember that women who became avowed feminists and were empowered to lead efforts at reform often faced painful choices. The Quaker meeting had supplied women a supportive environment for hearing a call to witness, but if that witnessing led a woman out of meeting, the group whose presence had been so significant for the calling no longer served for support. For that reason many leaders among women may be called only Quaker-related because they ceased, for their own or their meeting's reasons, being members of the Society of Friends. For those women, a husband like Stephen Foster, who shared isolation from meeting with his wife, proved a godsend. In Susan B. Anthony's case the Progressive Friends, of whom she had been a part, never relinquished their support, even after she resigned her membership. Others like Elizabeth Gray Vining, who traveled to Japan, were fortunate to keep a remnant of the Quaker community with them. But the message is clear: the dictates of conscience were too individual and disturbing to the norms of society for Quaker women to avoid separation from their communities at all times. Persevering in the face of isolation has often proved to be the most challenging trial in a Quaker woman's life course.

In conclusion, it is clear that the history of Quaker women deserves the attention historians have paid it. It is also clear that we have just begun the search for answers on the exceptional contributions of Quaker women. For this reason, the contributors to this volume believe it is important that readers become acquainted with the resources for studying Quaker women. Elisabeth Potts Brown of the Quaker Collection at Haverford College and Jean Soderlund, formerly of the Swarthmore College Peace Collection, have collaborated to tell us about the records left by Quaker women. They do this in expectation that interested readers will devote attention to these rich resource materials and in doing so deepen understanding of this unique history. For example, the Quaker

Collection at Haverford College includes material from both North America and England beginning in the seventeenth century. In the nineteenth and twentieth centuries it widens its scope to global records of Quaker women's roles. Brown and Soderlund review other collections of Quaker materials as well. The Swarthmore College Peace Collection is a special collection that includes materials from many centuries and countries, with major resources on twentieth-century women who worked for peace. These quiet records of heroism warrant our close attention.

The history of Quaker women is then both remarkable and inspiring, and only in its initial stages of development. By examining Quaker women we can learn what is necessary to move society beyond the restraints of debilitating gender ideology. We learn that women can effect the changes necessary to transform their social roles. We learn that for some women the cause of women's rights or world peace can become greater than the personal concerns of the advocate. Quaker women contributed their nonviolent methods to their causes, their belief that organizations should include people of all faiths and ethnic and racial groups. They contributed their skills at formulating goals and keeping records learned in Quaker meetings. They have left an inestimable legacy to us.

NOTES

1. E. William Monter, "Women in the Age of Reformations," in Renate Bridenthal, Claudia Koonz, and Susan Stuard, eds., *Becoming Visible* (Boston: Houghton Mifflin, 1987), 208.

2. "Witnesses for Change: Quaker Women 1650–1987," Haverford College, 6 April 1987. This is not the first conference that recognizes the importance of Quaker women. See the proceedings of a conference on Quaker women in American history held at Guilford College in 1978: Carol and John Stoneburner, eds., *The Influence of Quaker Women in American History* (Lewiston, N.Y.: Mellen, 1986).

3. Joan Kelly, *Women, History and Theory* (Chicago: University of Chicago Press, 1984), 56.

4. Bede, *A History of the English Church and People,* trans. L. Sherley-Price, rev. ed. (London: Dent, 1968), 245–250.

5. Bede's *Ecclesiastical History,* as it was familiarly called, was a national as well as a church treasure in England and survived Reformation efforts to suppress the popular lives of saints for that reason. In the north, where Quaker communities flourished in the seventeenth century, even a grammar school education (and many early Friends, particularly women Friends, never obtained more than this level of education) introduced Hild of Whitby to readers. Bede's stories were even included in grammar school readers. On literacy, see Hugh Barbour, *The Quakers in Puritan England* (New Haven: Yale Univer-

sity Press, 1964), 83, 132. Quaker women consciously chose Old Testament prophet-esses as their role models from close and careful reading of the Bible after they had undergone conversion. But at least the first generation of Quaker women was raised with the examples of the great early English saints before them as well.

6. *A Book of Showings to the Anchoress Julian of Norwich,* ed. E. Colledge and J. Walsh (Toronto: PIMS, 1978). Rufus Jones noted that "England [had] her Walter Hilton and Lady Julian," in *Studies in Mystical Religion* (London: Macmillan, 1909), 301, although he distinguished the "affirmative mysticism" of the seventeenth century "that was quite unlike a passage from Meister Eckhart or from the Lady Julian or any other fourteenth century mystic," in *Mysticism and Democracy in the English Commonwealth* (Cambridge: Harvard University Press, 1932), 14. However he goes on to argue, p. 16, that "the widespread pantheistic-mystical sects of the fourteenth century were never extermi-nated; they were rather driven down out of sight and became a submerged stream of influence." Thus Jones found a way to connect the mysticism of Julian of Norwich (who lived and wrote in the north like many of England's mystics and saints) with the resurgence of Quaker mysticism in the seventeenth century. Julian lived in popular memory, even when the veneration of saints was suppressed, as persistent local stories and associations attest.

7. The idea of Christ as mother was not new, however; St. Bernard had employed the same image in the twelfth century. See Caroline Bynum, *Christ as Mother* (Berkeley: University of California Press, 1982).

8. Betty Bandel, "The English Chroniclers' Attitude toward Women," *Journal of the History of Ideas,* 16 (1955): 113–118.

9. Gender is defined here as the system of relations between women and men.

10. Ian Maclean, *The Renaissance Notion of Woman* (Cambridge: Cambridge University Press, 1980). The full system of medieval polarities that were opposed and then aligned to reach a definition of woman were male: limit, odd, one, right, square, at rest, straight, light, and good; female: unlimited, even, plurality, left, oblong, moving, curved, darkness, evil. According to Maclean, these became commonplaces shared by the newly emerging disciplines of knowledge, but as unexplored assumptions rather than rigorously argued ideas, they merely came along in the train of more rigorously developed thought. Maclean believes the polar gender assumptions about women owe their long life to their notional quality and their status as unexamined commonplaces shared widely in medieval theology and other systems of thought.

11. Joan Kelly, "Did Women Have a Renaissance?" in Renate Bridenthal and Claudia Koonz, eds., *Becoming Visible,* 1st ed. (Boston: Houghton Mifflin, 1977). This article has been reprinted many times, including in the 1987 edition of *Becoming Visible.* Not all feminist interpretations follow Kelly's lead. Gerda Lerner in *The Creation of Patriarchy* (New York: Oxford, 1986) suggests the oppression of women was introduced with the emergence of ancient civilizations with their attendant wars and slavery and continues until today. Recently Riane Eisler, *The Chalice and the Blade: Our History, Our Future* (Cambridge, Mass.: Harper, 1987) argues for a complex pattern of two models of social organization from prehistory to the present: one male, rooted in force, and the other female, rooted in partnership. She sees something of her submerged second strand in the lives of religious women in early Europe. Elaine Pagels in *Gnostic Gospels* (New York: Random House, 1979) and *Adam, Eve and the Serpent* (New York: Random House, 1987) also finds a submerged empowering tradition for women in Christian doctrine originat-ing in the earliest Christian writings. (Genesis 1:3) Medievalists have responded to Pagels that some early medieval women in Europe were able to make use of that

empowering tradition. See Suzanne Wemple, *Women in Frankish Society* (Philadelphia: University of Pennsylvania Press, 1981) and her article with JoAnn McNamara in Mary Hartman and Lois Banner, eds., *Clio's Consciousness Raised* (New York: Harper & Row, 1974).

12. John Klassen, "Women and Religious Reform in Late Medieval Bohemia," *Renaissance and Reformation* 5:4 (1981): 203–221.

13. Martin Luther, *Werke, Kritische Gesamtausgabe* (Weimar, 1883), 42: 51–52.

14. E. William Monter, "Women in the Age of the Reformations," 203–219.

15. William Bouwsma, *John Calvin: A Sixteenth-Century Portrait* (New York: Oxford, 1987).

16. H. Kramer and J. Sprenger, *Malleus Maleficarum,* trans. Montague Summers (London: J. Rodker, 1928).

17. Keith Thomas, "Women in the Civil War Sects" *Past and Present* 13 (1958): 42–62.

18. E. William Monter, "Women in the Age of Reformations," 208.

19. Howard Brinton, *Friends for 300 Years* (New York: Harper, 1952), 11. On the early Quakers, see also Hugh Barbour and Arthur O. Roberts, eds., *Early Quaker Writings 1650–1700* (Grand Rapids: Eerdmans, 1973); William Braithwaite, *The Beginnings of Quakerism,* 2d ed., revised by Henry Cadbury (Cambridge: Cambridge University Press, 1955); Auguste Jorns, *The Quakers as Pioneers in Social Work,* trans. Thomas Kite Brown, Jr. (New York: Macmillan, 1931); Elfrida Vipont, *The Story of Quakerism, 1652–1952,* (London: Bannisdale, 1954); Mabel Richmond Brailsford, *Quaker Women, 1650–1690* (London: Duckworth, 1915); see also the notes that follow.

20. Hugh Barbour, *The Quakers in Puritan England,* 2. See also Geoffrey Nuttall, *The Holy Spirit in Puritan Faith and Experience* (Oxford: Basil Blackwell, 1946) 16–20.

21. Hugh Barbour, *Quakers in Puritan England,* 133. Barbour's understanding of early Quaker women is perhaps better seen in his "Quaker Prophetesses and Mothers in Israel," in J. William Frost and John M. Moore, eds., *Seeking the Light: Essays in Quaker History in Honor of Edwin B. Bronner* (Wallingford, Pa.: Pendle Hill Publications, and Haverford, Pa.: Friends Historical Association, 1986) 41–60.

22. For men, joining the Quaker sect meant being banned from Anglican Oxford and Cambridge universities on grounds of heterodoxy. Sons born to Quaker families could not attend these universities because of their religious affiliation.

23. George Fox, "An Encouragement to All Faithful Women's Meetings" (letter no. 320), in *The Works of George Fox,* vol. 8 (Philadelphia: Marcus Gould, 1831), 92–97, provides a good place to begin study of Fox's support of women in leadership roles in the Quaker community.

24. See document following the introduction. The Lancashire Women's Meeting in a letter circa 1675 to 1680 advocated that women both conduct monthly meetings and join with a broader circle of Quakers for a business meeting once a year.

25. Margaret Hope Bacon, *Mothers of Feminism* (San Francisco: Harper & Row, 1986) argues that the women's meetings for business sustained women's participation within the Society of Friends until they were integrated with men's in the 1920s. See also Mabel Richmond Brailsford, *Quaker Women, 1650–1690.*

26. Isabel Ross, *Margaret Fell, Mother of Quakerism* (London: Longmans Green, 1949), 302. See also note 25. The letter from the Lancashire Women's Meeting has been published as "A Seventeenth-Century Quaker Women's Declaration," transcribed with headnote by Milton D. Speizman and Jane C. Kronick in *SIGNS: Journal of Women in Culture and Society* 1:1 (1975): 231–245.

27. "A Seventeenth-Century Quaker Women's Declaration," 245.

28. Jean Soderlund, "Women's Authority in Pennsylvania and New Jersey Quaker Meetings, 1680–1760," *William and Mary Quarterly* 3:, 44 (1987): 722–749, examines in some detail the extent of women's independence in setting their own agendas and acting on them.

29. Margaret Hope Bacon, *Mothers of Feminism,* 39. Sydney James, in *A People among Peoples: Quaker Benevolence in Eighteenth-Century America* (Cambridge: Harvard University Press, 1963) takes a somewhat different view of this episode.

30. Margaret Hope Bacon, *Mothers of Feminism,* 71.

31. See, for example, J. William Frost, *The Quaker Family in Colonial America* (New York: St. Martins, 1973); Hugh Barbour, *The Quakers in Puritan England;* Digby Baltzell, *Puritan Boston and Quaker Philadelphia* (New York: Free Press, 1979); Judy Mann DiStefano, "The Concept of the Family in Colonial America. The Pembertons of Philadelphia" Ph.D. diss., Ohio State University, 1970, microfilm.

32. Mercedes Randall, *Improper Bostonian: Emily Greene Balch* (New York: Twayne, 1964).

DOCUMENT

Sometime between 1675 and 1680 this letter went out from the Lancashire Meeting of Women Friends to other women's meetings both sides of the Atlantic. This was very likely written by or under the guidance of Sarah Fell (1642–1714), the daughter of Margaret Fell. The letter gives justification for women's holding meeting and witnessing for their faith. It contains practical suggestions for how to carry on a Friend's meeting and it ends with a resounding call to battle in the name of faith. Only portions are included here. The full text is available, "A Seventeenth-Century Quaker Women's Declaration," transcribed with headnote by Milton D. Speizman and Jane C. Kronick, *Signs, Journal of Women in Culture and Society* 1:1 (1975) 231–245 (published by University of Chicago Press). This was the first publication of this important letter, although copies may be found in collections of Quaker records in both England and North America.

From our Country Women's meeting in Lancashire to be Dispersed abroad, among the Women's meetings every where.

Dear Sisters.

    In the blessed unity in the Spirit of grace our Souls Salute you who are sanctified in Christ Jesus, and called to be Saints. God sent forth his Son made of a woman, made under the Law to redeem them that were under the [Law?] that we might receive adoption. To you all every where, where this may come, is this written; that in this blessed seed, which hath the promise of the eternal God, that he should bruise the serpents head, and that in his seed you all live and dwell in the sensible feeling thereof, in which seed all nations of the earth is blessed: that so we may be all helps meet for God in the restoration, and co-heires with Christ Jesus, who hath purchased us with his precious bloud, and who hath washed us and loved us, who is no respecter of persons, but hath a care, and a regard unto all, the weak as well as the strong, that he may have the glory of his own work, who treadeth the wine-press alone. And that every particular of us, may be ready, and willing to answer what the lord requires of us; in our several places and conditions; for as many of us are baptized into Christ, have put on Christ; for we are all children of God by faith in Christ Jesus, where there is neither male nor female &c. but we are all one in Christ Jesus. . . .

And let us meet together, and keep our womens meetings, in the name and power, and fear of the lord Jesus, whose servants and handmaids we are, and in the good order of the Gospel meet.

1st   And first, for the women of every of every [*sic*] monthly meeting, where the mens monthly meetings is established, let the women likewise of every monthly meeting, meet together to wait upon the lord, and to hearken what the lord will say unto them, and to know his mind, and will, and be ready to obey, and answer him in every motion of his eternal spirit and power.

2ly   And also, to make inquiry into all your severall particular meetings, that belongs to your monthly meetings, If there be any that walks disorderly, as does not become the Gospell, or lightly, or wantonly, or that is not of a good reporte: Then send to them, as you are ordered by the power of God in the meeting, (which is the authority of it) to Admonish, and exhort them, and to bring them to Judge, and Condemn, what hath been by them done or acted contrary to the truth.

3ly   And if any transgression or Action that hath been done amongst women or maids, that hath been more publick, and that hath gott into the world, or that hath been a publick offence among friends; then let them bring in a paper of condemnation, to be published as far, as the offence hath gone, and then to be recorded in a booke.

4th   And if there be any that goes out to Marry, with priests, or joineth in Marriage with the world, and does not obey the order of the Gospell as is established amongst friends, then for the womens month meeting to send to them, to reprove them, and to bear their testimony against their actions.

5ly   And also all friends that keeps in the power of God, and in faithful obedience to the truth, that according to the order of the Gospell that is established, that they bring their Marriages twice to the women meetings and twice to the mens. . . .

6ly   And likewise, that the women of the monthly meetings take and oversight of all the women that belongs to their several parish meetings, that they bring in their testimonies for the lord, and his flock against tithes, and hireling priests once every yeare. . . .

7ly   And at every monthly meeting, that they give timely notice, to every regular meeting, that they make ready their testimonies against tithes brought in at other Quarterly meeting . . . that all hearts and consciences may be kept cleare, clean and sweet, to our serious high priest of our profession, who is the Author of our Faith. . . .

8ly   And also all friends, in their womens monthly, and particular Meetings that they take special care for the poore, and for those that stand in need.

And that all the sick, and weak, and Infirme, or Aged, and widdows, and fatherless, that they be looked after, and helped, and relieved, in the particular meeting, either with clothes, or maintainance, or what they stand in need off.

9ly   Also let Care be taken that every particular womens monthly meeting have a booke to set down, and record their bussinesses and passages that is done or agreed upon, in every monnethly meeting, or any task that any is to go upon, let the book be read, the next monthly meeting, and see that the business be performed, according to what was entered.

And also that the collections be set downe, in the booke; and that the Receipts, and disbursments of every particular meeting, be set down in their book, and read at their womens monthly meeting, that every particular meeting may see and know, how their collections is disbursed.

And that some faithfull honest woman, or women friends, that can Read, and write, keep the Book and receive the Collections, and give just and a true account, of the disbursments of them in the book, according as the meeting shall order, which must be Read every month meeting; And so give notice what is in stock; and when it is near out, to give notice that it may be supplyed.

10ly [Tells how meetings are to be scheduled throughout the year]

And though wee be looked upon as the weaker vessels, yet strong and powerfull is God, whose strength is made perfect in weakness, he can make us good and bold, and valliant Souldiers of Jesus Christ, if he arm us with his Armour of Light, and give unto us the sword of his Eternal God, and cover our hearts with the breast-plate of righteousness, and crown us with the helmet of salvation, and give unto us the Shield of Faith, with which we can quench all the firey darts of Sathan. . . .

This is given forth for Information, Instruction, and Direction, that in the blessed unity of the spirit of grace, all friends may bee, and live in the practice of the holy order of the Gospell; if you know these things, happy are you if ye do them so.

ONE

The Seventeenth Century

PHYLLIS MACK

Gender and Spirituality in Early English Quakerism, 1650–1665

W HEN OLD Elizabeth Hooton became the first person in England to preach the doctrines of the Quaker George Fox, her neighbors in the village of Skegby were probably not very much surprised. The wife of a prosperous farmer and mother of four grown children, Hooton was already a teacher in her local Baptist community when she first encountered Fox, and it was she, not her husband Oliver, who took the lead in converting to Quakerism. Thrown into prison as a disturber of the peace in the early 1650s, she became an aggressive agitator against the corruption of clergy and magistrates. "You make yourselves ridiculous to all people who have sense and reason," she wrote. "Your judges judge for reward, and . . . many which committed murder escaped through friends and money, and poor people for lesser facts are put to death. . . . They lie [in prison] worse than dogs for want of straw."[1]

She seemed to be without terror of any worldly authority. When her husband died, she proceeded to embark on a missionary voyage to America, where she offended magistrates and ministers in New England by returning to preach again and again and again, after being stripped, whipped from town to town, and abandoned in the forests. Once she and a pregnant friend reached their destination by following a track through the woods that had been made in the snow by a wolf. In 1662, again in England, she harangued King Charles II in a state of such ecstacy and audacity that she was said by some to be a witch:

The power of the lord was risen in me . . . and some wicked ones said that it was of the devil and some present made answer and said they wish they had that spirit, and then they were my disciples . . . the Lord . . . made me an instrument to make way . . . so is the lord now filling up his viols of wrath to pour on the throne of the beast.[2]

An established leader of her own local meeting, Hooton also traveled and suffered with other female missionaries, most notably her own daughter; yet she was a woman who made exuberant use of the traditional stock of vicious antifemale metaphors. In her "Lamentation for Boston and Cambridge her Sister," she wrote,

by your unrighteous decrees hatched at Cambridge and made at Boston you are the two breasts of New England where all Cruelty is nursed up, . . . and by these two breasts they are blood suckers persecuters and murderers. . . . (God) will rend and tear and deliver His little ones out of your hands, and shake terribly, and put out your two eyes.[3]

She was an ascetic who wrote to friends of the need to suffer continually, but she was also protective of her own considerable possessions—her house, lands and cattle. In several letters to the king, she requested that he restore her property to her, "that I may have a horse to ride on in my old age."[4]

Visiting Barbados and Jamaica in 1672, her third missionary voyage across the Atlantic, Hooton exhorted the Quaker settlers to sustain their faith. One of those Friends, James Lancaster, remembered that the next day,

she was much swelled, and I said let her have air and they opened the windows and opened her bodice and then her breath came and she looked up and see me but could not speak . . . and she looked upon me and I her . . . and she said it is well James thou art come and fastened her arms about me . . . and embraced me with a kiss and laid her self Down and turned her self on her side and so her breath went weaker and weaker till it was gone from her and so passed away as though she had been asleep and none knew of her departure but as her breath was gone.[5]

THE CONTEMPORARIES of Elizabeth Hooton would have agreed that there was no truer Quaker than that old woman, though her daughter Elizabeth and her antagonists, the magistrates and ministers of Boston, would surely have had different images of Quakerism in mind when they said the words. Most audiences were impressed, above all, by the extraordinary zeal and audacity of the more than two hundred Quaker women who prophesied during the early years of the movement.[6] Among the first missionaries in Ireland was a woman, Elizabeth Fletcher, sixteen years old, who arrived in 1655. The first missionaries to America were women, Mary Fisher and Anne Austin, who preached in Barbados in 1655 and arrived in Boston in 1656. The first and only missionary to Turkey was a woman, Mary Fisher, who walked alone five hundred miles to visit the Sultan; face to face with the tyrant, she announced that he was the one man in Europe most in need of her message. The youngest and oldest Quakers to preach in public during the 1650s were female: Mary Fell of Swarthmore told the local Anglican priest, "Lampitt the plagues of god shall fall upon thee and the seven viols shall be poured upon thee, and the milstone shall fall upon thee and crush thee as dust under the Lord's feet how can thou escape the damnation of hell." Mary Fell was eight. Elizabeth Hooton admonished the king in the words of a reproving parent: "How often have I come to thee in my old age, both for thy reformation and safety, for the good of thy soul, and for justice and equity." She was about seventy.[7]

For other, more sympathetic observers, the essence of the Quakers' uniqueness seemed to lie, not in personal audacity, but its opposite; the physical and emotional restraint of even its most charismatic leaders. The magistrates who flinched at Elizabeth Hooton's invectives would never have characterized her testimony as one of passive resistance, but Quakers saw themselves as excelling in precisely that; they sought verbal confrontations with clergy and magistrates and submitted to the inevitable persecution, in order to dramatize the contrast between their own apostolic innocence and the magistrates' unenlightened souls, and they did this even before pacifism had become the official policy of the movement after 1660.[8] Certainly women like Elizabeth Hooton were champions of heroic endurance. Not only did they attempt more exotic journeys than their male counterparts; they also suffered more theatrically than men, if only because the sight of a woman stripped to the waist and bound to a whipping post, clasping her baby to her naked chest, must have had a different social and sexual resonance than the sight of a man in the same cruel position.

Whatever their degree of sympathy for the tenets and practices of early Quakerism, audiences were in no doubt that Quaker women had departed from the conventions of acceptable feminine behavior far more radically than was the case for the visionaries who spoke and wrote before them or alongside them. Those other women—women like Anna Trapnel and Sarah Wight or the anonymous maidens who returned from the dead to advise the living— may have carried conventional female behavior to extremes, but they were recognizable and acceptable as women nonetheless; feminine in their exaggerated susceptibility to trances and emotional outbursts, in their use of images of motherhood and whoredom to convey their visionary insights, and above all in their physical passivity, even catatonia, as they enlightened their audiences by their predictions and spiritual counseling.

Elizabeth Hooton also used gendered images of virgins, mothers, and whores to praise the righteous and castigate the unjust, but there her resemblance to other, non-Quaker visionary women ended. For the Quaker prophet did not act out of the popular tradition of pagan divination; she was not an oracle, like a sort of spiritual battery, humming with the invisible energy of the universe. On the contrary, the Quaker prophet was an active messenger out of the pages of the Old Testament. Her duty was to initiate direct encounters, to teach hard truths, to condemn moral decadence and social injustice, and, above all, to warn the sinner "that God may be justified in his judgements."[9]

In assuming the personae of biblical prophets, Quaker women seemed to be denying the reality of all outward cultural constraints. They denied class and status differences by refusing to use the verbal or body language of deference; they denied gender differences by insisting that they preached as disembodied spirits "in the light," not as women. Indeed, if Quaker women prophets could be said to resemble any cultural archetype, it was that of the aggressive, male Old Testament hero.

What were the deeper reasons for Elizabeth Hooton's unorthodox, unfeminine behavior? Some have viewed the ecstatic preaching of visionary women as a form of emotional catharsis and a symptom of women's fundamental psychic instability, a view stated explicitly by the historian Ronald Knox:

The history of enthusiasm is largely a history of female emancipation, and it is not a reassuring one. [Indeed] . . . the sturdiest champion of women's rights will hardly deny that the unfettered exercise of the prophetic ministry by the more devout sex can threaten the ordinary decencies of ecclesiastical order.[10]

Other scholars have expressed the same, negative perception in more subtle, possibly unconscious ways: According to David Lovejoy, Anne Hutchinson did not *think* about religious issues— she "soaked up" antinomianism; in William Braithwaite's classic study of the beginnings of Quakerism, no women's writings are mentioned except those of Margaret Fell, but every case of "light behavior" by a woman is described in detail; in Christopher Hill's innovative work, *The World Turned Upside Down,* the sympathetic discussion of women in the radical sects occurs only in the chapters on insanity and free love.[11]

Historians of women generally disagree with these writers' perceptions about the causes of women's emotional frustration, but they tend to agree that religious women preached in order to fulfill nonreligious needs. Confined to an obscure existence, without property, official power, or political status, visionary women supposedly experienced a sense of freedom and self-realization when they spoke in public; in lieu of opportunities elsewhere, they made a career of preaching, in the modern sense of the word "career." Historian Mabel Brailsford tells the story of the Quaker Judith Zinspinning, whose father was often heard to regret that she had not been born a boy, so as to become an eminent figure in the church. While married, her "buried talent and stifled ambition revenged themselves in moods of discontent and morbid introspection." As soon as her husband died, she sent her only son to live with an uncle and began a career as a famous, and presumably more fulfilled polemicist and preacher.[12]

These approaches to the subject of women's spirituality are emphatically opposed in their conclusions, but they rest, nonetheless, on two identical assumptions about the meaning of female behavior: The first is that women used a religious vocabulary to express needs which were, at bottom, nonreligious; the second is that the place to look for the true shape of these needs and desires is in overt demonstrations of aggression and emotion. I would like to take issue with both of these assumptions, and to argue that the Quakers' most passionate, apparently willful behavior was not an expression of their deepest personal desires; nor was their public assertiveness actually a form of self-expression—whether interpreted as uncontrolled hysteria or as a gesture of defiance, of oppressed women trying to act like men. For the Quakers' attitude toward the self differed radically from the one that dominates our own, late-twentieth-century western culture, informed by fairly rigid standards of self-control and self-integration. Modern Freudian and post-Freudian theory, progressive children's literature, popular how-to-do-it books on love, hobbies or making money—all these artifacts of our society teach us, with varying degrees of subtlety, that a mature, self-aware personality or ego is the foundation that supports the entire edifice of one's emotional, sexual, and spiritual being. We view the ego or conscious self as a sort of command center, mediating between conscience (or superego), the internalized voice of the larger culture, and instinct (or id), the hidden, volatile inner core of the self. Without a strong, independent ego and a firmly orchestrated personality (in contemporary slang, 'having it all together'), one becomes, at best, a mediocrity in a society that values independence and achievement, and at worst, a professional failure, a social and moral cripple, a hopeless neurotic, even insane.

Within this psychological framework, emotional behavior does appear as a loosening of outward habits of control, the individual's deep, hidden essence spilling out. If we come upon a man or woman in a crowded city street, shouting or weeping loudly, clothes disheveled, we assume that we are witnessing an act of greater personal intimacy than that of a man or woman in a neat business suit, writing a check or giving an order in a restaurant. We might also assume that such behavior is a bypassing of the superego, the self erupting through the constraints of the culture, either through indifference to one's surroundings and to potential embarrassment (a mother wailing over the body of her dead child after an earthquake), or in conscious defiance of conventional standards of behavior (an audience at a rock concert).

The Quakers' conception of the self turns our modern archaeology of the personality virtually upside down. Quakers viewed all human drives or appetites as superficial and transitory, those things that pass away with the death of the individual, and they included in this the drive to satisfy the cravings of the intellect as well as those of the stomach and the genitals. They further believed that the deepest, most hidden, most authentic aspect of the self was divine love and knowledge of both nature and ethics; a knowledge of which our own conscience, or superego, is a pale shadow. For the Quakers' conscience was a shard of universal truth, God's voice imbedded in the self, which they called "the light" or "the seed."

In the act of preaching, that light or voice of conscience was catapulted from the depths of the soul, through layers of temperament, appetite and habit, finally bursting through the individual's outer husk—her social status, her physical shape, her gender—to unite with the voices of other Friends in prayer or to enlighten strangers in the public arena. Unlike other visionaries, the Quaker prophet was not in a trance when she preached—her whole being on hold, so to speak—for the voice of God was also the voice of her own conscience or integrity, the light within, or rather beneath, her deepest self, which put her in harmony with universal moral truth. Thus Jane Withers advised readers that she was not in a trance when she entered a church to berate the minister:

The power of God seized upon me, . . . that I was bound about my body above the middle as if . . . with chains. . . . And in the afternoon, I was forced to go (into the church), . . . and then the power of the Lord came upon me; but if that priest Moore says, I was in a trance, it is a lie, for I was as sensible all the while as ever I was.[13]

Quaker women also sincerely argued, in terms which were only apparently contradictory, that they were not being assertive when they preached; on the contrary, they were actually preaching against their own wills and minds. Margaret Killam recalled (typically writing in the passive tense), "I was made to go into church. They said I was subtle, but I was was kept in innocency, and found nothing rising in me til [the minister] was down. I was made in meekness to declare truth."[14]

Thus Quaker prophecy both was and was not an expression of the prophet's individual character; it was emphatically not a spontaneous outpouring of mood or individual imagination. On the contrary, the Quakers' confidence that their preaching emanated from God and not the devil or mere ego, was based largely on the resemblance of their own words and gestures to the traditional language of biblical figures. When Katherine Evans declared that "whatsoever I have written, it's not because it is recorded in the Scripture, . . . but in obedience to the Lord I have written the things which I did hear, see, tasted and handled of the good word of God," she did not mean that her own revelations were independent of the Bible, but that God had made her feel Him in the same way, and with the same words, that He had spoken to biblical prophets. (Indeed, the phrase "hear, see, tasted and handled" was itself a quotation from the Bible).[15] Quaker preachers thus assumed the existence of a shared mnemonic culture, a range of symbols and actions whose meaning would be universally understood, and whose power, they hoped, would be universally acknowledged.

In 1679, Judith Boulbie wrote to the people of Ireland, in words close to those of Jeremiah:

My bowels are troubled, I am pained as one to be delivered, or as one whom wine hath overcome, because of the Lord. . . . the Lord God will strike off your chariot-wheels, and that which is the joy, and comfort and satisfaction of God's people, will be your woe and torment; it will be in you as a worm that will never die, it will gnaw you in your inward parts, and it will be in you as a fire that can never be quenched.[16]

Of course the language of Judith Boulbie and Elizabeth Hooton was emotional, and the intensity of their public voices, which hostile contemporaries described as shouting or screaming, may well have held a residue of personal frustration or exultation; more importantly, it was an expression of the prophet's ritually expressed anguish over the nation, mediated through the conventional language and behavior of biblical figures.[17] Indeed, we shall see that it was precisely in their most passionate and aggressive aspect, hurling invectives at magistrates and clergy, that Quaker women visionaries appear to have been the most constrained and unoriginal as individuals, while the more emotional women— those who *did* express their personal feelings in their writings or who were judged by other Quakers to be excessive or self-serving in their public behavior—actually preached less.

And yet, having affirmed the centrality of the Quakers' spiritual concerns and observed an affinity between Quaker styles of expression and that of biblical figures—having, as it were, pleaded for the soul as a category of historical analysis—one comes back to the question of personal motivation: Why imitate *these* biblical figures, and not others? Why make *these* symbolic gestures, and not others? Why do *these* women convert, write, and preach and not others? And if public preaching was not a mode of self-expression for most Quaker women, were there other aspects of the experience of "the light" that *did* provide a measure of personal fulfillment to those who were convinced?

One also comes back to the question of the meaning of gender. A primary tenet of early Quakerism was that the hierarchical character of gender relationships, indeed of all social relationships, was a product of human sinfulness, an outcome of the original Fall from Grace. That Fall had shattered humanity into fragments, and the placement of those fragments, far from reflecting the moral and aesthetic unity of a universal chain of being, were unnatural and imperfect forms of expression and oppression, social hierarchies that were to be overcome through the painful annihilation of the outward self. But Quakers lived and proselytized in a society where the language of social roles and moral values was completely gendered; where in biblical tradition, every transgression was expressed in metaphors of wifely infidelity and every soul in anguish as a woman in labor; where, in political discourse, the most antisocial crime was perceived as female witchcraft and the pinnacle of social harmony as the king or familial patriarch. In such an atmosphere, speaking and writing in a culture where one strove to be at least partially at home, it would have been impossible to communicate the meaning of the Quaker's rebirth "in the light" or the warnings of an angry God, and avoid using the language of masculine and feminine.

In the remainder of this essay, I want to analyze the meaning of gender to early Quaker women and men in terms of the Quakers' personal and religious expectations, both in this world and out of it. What motive caused Elizabeth Hooton to leave her own prosperous farm in order to expose herself and her daughter, and other old women, to the hazards of the American wilderness, inhabited by

39

savage, ungodly Puritans? Was it the same motive as that of male Quakers who made similar sacrifices and faced similar dangers? How did a people whose aim was to transcend the limitations of their outward circumstance, including differences of gender, come to terms with the gendered discourse of the larger culture, and how did they attempt to shape that discourse to their own ends, or rather, to godly, spiritual ends? Why did the female leaders of a sexually egalitarian movement, speak with the voice of male biblical figures, and not those of Deborah or Esther or Miriam? What was the mentality that allowed Quaker women to be both tender and abrasive, mothers in Israel and scourges to humble the unrighteous? In short, from the limited perspective of modern scholarship and imagination, observing the earliest Quakers at this vast temporal and cultural distance, I want to trace the linaments of Elizabeth Hooton's human and spiritual shape.

Ecstacy and Community

From the post–Enlightenment perspective of many modern historians, the key, often pejorative word for the troubles of the mid–seventeenth century is "enthusiasm": impulsive, emotional behavior involving a loss of reason and self-control. For seventeenth-century Quakers, 'enthusiasm' was also a dirty word, but not because it implied a *loss* of selfhood; on the contrary, it conveyed a sense of self-generated, self-centered, willful energy. In both the flamboyant behavior of contemporary groups like the Ranters and the more sedate, intellectual preaching of the Anglican and Puritan clergy, Quakers saw the self run rampant. For these Quakers, both will and mind were, quite simply, the enemies of the soul, and the first object of Quaker meditation, prayer, good deeds, or visions was to suffocate impulses toward personal expression and achieve the annihilation of the thinking self. "Dwell low in God," wrote Elizabeth Hendricks, "Feel the lamb that suffers. Don't run ahead of God. Keep your mind clean of reasonings. . . . Watch against those who want to understand."[18]

In order to appreciate this relentless self-negation in terms the early Quakers would have understood, we must begin by admitting that our own life goals of happiness, self-respect, and individual self-expression would have seemed to them to be both deluded and trivial. Quakers aimed for nothing less than the experience of God's presence, or indwelling, in their own bodies; they also wanted friendship and spiritual unity with the entire community of Quakers; ultimately, they even wanted to conquer death. As Mary Howgill put it to Oliver Cromwell: "We are all soldiers against all sin and deceit, and have overcome death, hell, and the grave."[19]

Such exalted feats of self-transformation were not achieved through the mere intellectual comprehension of a particular set of doctrines or the satisfaction of personal, worldly success. Not only was intellectual activity a dangerous pastime, encouraging the sin of pride and the idolatry of the Anglican priests, it was also simply irrelevant to the existential experience Quakers sought. One male Quaker who felt the call to speak at a meeting and was afraid, forced himself to think about the subject and immediately the spirit left him. "I saw I could do nothing, having quenched the spirit," he wrote, "and I was under trouble and exercise for my disobedience."[20] When the intellectual Judith Zinspinning arrived from Holland to preach in England, she intended to use a translator, but the Quakers asked her to preach in Dutch even though they could not understand a word she said. They knew well that the prophet's deeper message was nonsense; literally non-sense.[21] In many Quakers' actual conversion experience, it was words—the seducers of the mind—not the flesh, which proved to be the real whore, because the enjoyment of one's own wisdom and eloquence fed the carnal appetite for self-esteem long after the other appetites of the body had been subdued. "I ran forth in my wisdom comprehending the mysteries of God," wrote Edward Burrough, ". . . and I grew up into Notion, to talk of high things . . . and my delight was much in discoursing, where I played the harlot . . . here I was run from my Husband after other Lovers."[22]

The Quakers' annihilation of pride and appetite was never viewed as an end in itself, however. On the contrary, the emptying of the self-made space in both mind and body that was then suffused from within by divine light; that same light, or seed, which had lain buried under layers of personality and habit. Not surprisingly, Quakers trusted the language of the body more than that of words, to demonstrate the authenticity of this spiritual rebirth.[23] The Quakers' particular style of physical expression, their quaking, was also a social statement, a commentary on the body language of their contemporaries. For Quakers lived in a world where many of the physical gestures of affection, association, deference, and punishment—kissing, eating, bowing, whipping, and the range of emotions that accompanied them—were often more closely associated with public ritual and convention than with individual feeling or impulse.[24] The Quakers repudiated all such gestures of deference and oppression, and their displays of tears, symbolic dress and undress, partial paralysis, and involuntary quaking were clear statements that they had divorced themselves from all corrupt habits of social ritual, self-glorification, or control.

Perhaps the Quakers' physical quaking was also resonant of the uninhibited, involuntary motions of infancy. Like many of their contemporaries, Quakers perceived the experience of salvation as the bliss of babyhood, the soul eating or sucking God's word as milk, or the soul as a seed, nestled and burgeoning under God's maternal wing, cradled and safe from the unreal individuation and loneliness of the carnal world.

The symbolic and emotional focus of this experience of blissful infancy were the parental figures of Margaret Fell and George Fox, whose relationship to Quakers was portrayed in terms of a fluidity that was both erotic and maternal, with images of mutual penetration, holding, and feeding, all derived from biblical language. "My life flows into thee," wrote Richard Hubberthorn to George Fox. "The world knows thee not but I know thee and feel thee . . . thy eye pearceth through me and is as the Arrows of god within me . . . I am broken into unfeigned tears."[25] John Audland cried to Margaret Fell, "O my dear sister my mother my well beloved one my life my Joy, I read thee daily thou art bound up in me . . . breathe to me more and more and I shall feel thee I am open to thee my most dear sister glorious is thy dwelling place."[26]

The Quakers' doctrine of perfection and feminine spiritual symbolism obviously had a positive impact on women's confidence as interpreters of the divine will, and as actors in the divine cause. From the Quakers' own perspective, however, the importance of the doctrine of perfection was not only, or even primarily, in granting authority to individual women, but in what one might call its liquifying aspect, its potential for loosening definitions of gender and encouraging women and men to speak and act with the traditional attributes of both sexes. Thus, George Fox was portrayed as being "so meek, contented, modest, easy, steady, tender, it was a pleasure to be in his company . . . [he] experienced no authority but over evil, and that . . . with love, compassion, and long suffering."[27] Margaret Fell, on the other hand, was addressed not only as bride, mother, and sister, but as hero and friend: "Arise thou daughter of Zion," wrote Thomas Aldam. "Thresh o Thresh upon the mountains; stand up for the Everlasting truth. The sword is put into thy hand; go forth in the strength of the lord as he calls, sit not still when the Lord bids go. . . . Thy appearance . . . in that which is Eternal, is to Judge."[28] Indeed, Quaker private correspondence often conveys the sense that the early Friends' emotional and spiritual lives were conducted in a sort of gravity-free zone, in which relationships attained a fluidity impossible to achieve "in the flesh." When the minister of a country church quoted St. Paul's injunction against women preaching to the prophet Dewens Morry, "she denied that it was the voice of a woman who spoke, but said that it was the voice of the spirit of God."[29] John Perrot signed a letter to the Quakers, "I am your Sister in our Spouse, John."[30]

WHILE FREEDOM from selfhood liberated Quaker men to use the verbal and body language of feminity and infancy in their intimate relations with the group, it liberated Quaker women to use the verbal and body language of masculine authority in their public prophecies. Women addressed magistrates, clergymen and monarchs, face to face, in churches, graveyards, and before the doors of Parliament. They published speeches, visions, and theological works which they sold on streetcorners and in front of taverns. They traveled, usually in pairs, across Europe, eastern America and the Caribbean, in imitation of Old Testament prophets and New Testament apostles. Thus, we find that the same people who expressed themselves privately as sucking infants, as the bride in the Song of Songs, or as admirers of the spiritual motherhood of Margaret Fell, presented themselves in public as virtual incarnations of angry male biblical prophets; God the mother, the hen protecting her baby chicks, was transformed, in the public arena, into God as a thundering, judgmental patriarch, chastizing the unregenerate Israelites (that is, the wicked of England) as whores and unfaithful wives.

In analyzing the quality and emotional authenticity of the Quakers' visionary language, we must remember that the private letters of Ann Audland and Mary Howgill were no more personal or creative than their public rhetoric, for both their handwritten letters and their published tracts were ultimately derived from the traditional imagery of the Bible.[31] The point is rather that Quakers, both women and men, felt impelled to identify themselves with feminine biblical images in their private and communal aspect, and impelled to identify themselves as masculine, Old Testament prophets when they assumed authority before the gaze of the outside world. Mary Howgill drew on a specific cultural archetype when she wrote privately to Margaret Fell, "Dear mother in the everlasting fountain of life I dearly salute thee and my love runs forth to thee daily in the unity of life which the lord hath called us unto into. . . . My soul is nourished and refreshed daily by that which is eternal. . . . I rest thy dear sister in that which never changes."[32] She drew on another cultural archetype when, during the same period, she addressed a letter to the people of England: "You are found in Idolatry, and the mother of that Idolatry is a whore. . . . Your gay and glorious clothing, its of your selves, and of the whorish woman, which hath the cup of abomination in her hand, and you are found in an ill smell, stinking in the nostrils of God."[33]

Just as men sometimes dressed as women to express the triumph of disorder in riots or charivaris, so Quaker women behaved like men when they appeared in marketplaces, churches, and graveyards to address the unregenerate.[34] Indeed, for women whose thinking had been shaped within a thoroughly patriarchal culture, it was authentic, completely in tune with their own personal and cultural experience, to express their public authority in the language of male prophets; whatever their specific background or personal temperament, women woke up at night with the words of Jonah and Jeremiah ringing in their heads. When the adolescent Elizabeth Andrews preached to the aristocrats who had been her family's patrons, and they proposed to 'rescue' her by making her a lady in waiting, she shot back, "Moses, the Servant of the Lord, refused to be called the son of Pharoah's Daughter, but rather chose to suffer affliction with the people of God than to enjoy the pleasures of sin . . . and so had I."[35]

What kind of woman had the audacity to lecture her social betters as Elizabeth Andrews and Elizabeth Hooton did? There is certainly no evidence that women converted and preached because they were more socially oppressed or personally frustrated than their neighbors; on the contrary, many were already more powerful within their families and neighborhoods than their peers. Margaret Fell's position on her estate of Swarthmore was less subservient than that of many other gentlewomen of the period; her husband tolerated her conversion and her use of their house for large meetings even though he never converted himself, and later, when she and George Fox married, they shocked contemporaries by drawing up a marriage contract so that her independent property would remain hers. Elizabeth Hooton was a leader in her Baptist community; later, as a widow, she controlled her property, and travelled as a missionary against the advice of her adult son. Women addressed the king and parliament not just because they were in an ecstatic state, but because they had access to these men through personal connections; Martha Simmonds, for instance, was the nurse to the sister of Oliver Cromwell. Certainly Quaker women were more literate than average; even if their writings were occasionally copied by other hands, they were still readers of the Bible and of each others' tracts. In short, either Quaker women preachers were more educated and powerful than many of their contemporaries, or our received wisdom about marriage and family life in early modern England needs to be reconsidered and revised.[36]

The most important single element affecting the writing and behavior of Quaker women—more important by far than the facts of age, economic and social position, marital status, motherhood, or education—was geography. The acts of preaching, writing, and suffering seemed to represent a different challenge for women of the rural, northern counties of Yorkshire, Lancashire, or Westmoreland, than they did for those of the more urbanized counties of the south. Northern women were more physically and verbally aggressive; they made more hazardous and repeated missionary journeys, and they wrote with greater anger and a more militant class consciousness. Thus spoke Margaret Killam, sister of a farmer from Yorkshire:

Howl ye rich men . . . for the rust of your Silver and Gold shall eat you through as a canker. . . . Wo to you that have fed your-selves with the fat, and clothed your selves with the wool, and the people perish for want of knowledge; . . . I will spread dung on your faces, yes I have cast dung on your faces already.[37]

Old Testament rhetoric was, of course, a characteristic of all Quaker writing; but in writings of women from the cities of the south, their public language was sometimes tempered by a gentler, more mystical and introspective tone, and a greater emotional range and self-absorption, often expressed in feminine imagery. The London writer, Dorothy White, used biblical imagery in a fashion that was less punitive, more lyrical, and more self-consciously artistic, than the language of female prophets from the north. The "I" of her prose is not God's voice (as in Margaret Killam's "I have cast dung in your faces already"); it is openly her own voice. "And the Lord God hath spoken," she wrote, "and therefore I will speak":

The *dissolving Power* of the Lord God, is dissolving *Hell* and *Death;* . . . and this is the Birth which is brought forth through the *Travail,* through *Death,* . . . for the *Bridegroom* is come, the *Virgins* have *met* him, and the *Damosels* dance at the glory of his *Brightness,* . . . for the *ravishing* Glory of God did overshadow me . . . whose Life hath filled me, . . . And in the deep his voice is very sweet . . . and unto my Beloved, unto Thee, I sweetly sing.[38]

However, while the behavior of northern women was certainly more aggressive than that of southern prophets (aggression directed inward, toward the self, and outward, toward the unregenerate), it was also less problematic for the women themselves. Northern women sought and endured more physical punishment than women from the south, but they also worried less. Whereas northern women like Elizabeth Hooton did not acknowledge any difficulty in renouncing the comforts of ordinary life, southern women were painfully aware of the material and intellectual sacrifices required by their conversion. Even after their convincement, southern women continued to be more self-absorbed and occasionally more concerned about the source of their public spiritual authority, than women from the north. So Elizabeth Adams of Kent, having ridden through Canterbury with a burning torch in her hand, wrote to George Fox, "I hope thou need not be ashamed of me, but if I have misbehaved my self in any thing as concerning the truth, if thou have a word from the lord, dear friend, deal plainly with me."[39] Indeed, the most unsettled and emotional women—those who disrupted meetings, engaged in personal feuds, or exaggerated either their own authority or that of other Quakers—came predominantly from the south.[40]

How can we account for this considerable difference in the language and activity of early Quaker women? Northern prophets, of whom Elizabeth Hooton was a clear archetype, were products of a relatively isolated, rural, austere, class-conscious, and intensely biblical culture; indeed, many northern women were veterans of Bible-study or Seeker groups before the arrival of Quakerism.[41] No wonder their prose was more monochromatic, and their awareness of social injustice, particularly the imposition of tithes, so much more pronounced. There was also less cultural dissonance between their previous experience as farmers and religious Seekers, and their adoption of Old Testament rhetoric and behavior; as Amos and Hosea strode out of the desert to castigate the decadent Jews of the cities, so Margaret Killam and Ann Audland strode out of the moors and fens of the north to castigate the decadent Christians of London and Bristol. The lives of most southern women, on the other hand, were conducted within a more complex, urbanized culture. Southern prophets were married to tradesmen, artisans, or publishers; they were relatively well educated, with access to mystical literature imported from the Continent and published by their own families. They were also exposed to many more forms of religious expression before their conversion to Quakerism, including the preaching of other female visionaries; the non-Quaker prophets Anna Trapnel, Sarah Wight, Eleanor Davies, Eleanor Channel, and Mary Cary all lived in or near London, and all prophesied to the same London audiences.[42]

The evident confusion experienced by many southern women about the source of their public spiritual authority was not only a consequence of their specific cultural environment; it was also the inevitable consequence of the dictates of their theology. For the terms on which Quaker women preached were very different from those that animated other, contemporary visionary women. The spiritual authority of Anna Trapnel and Sarah Wight rested on their feminine propensity to fall into trances and absorb spiritual influences, while the authority of Martha Simmonds or Elizabeth Hooton rested on the fact that, during the time that she preached, she was not a woman at all. True, some Quakers *did* defend their public acts by citing the ancient Christian tradition of paradox, which held that the last—the poor, the ignorant, the diseased and despised—shall ultimately be first.[43] Quakers also argued that, when a woman was in the light, she was God's bride, "at home" and in her proper place in the sense of being obedient to God, entirely passive and speaking only in His voice, even though her carnal self appeared to be screaming at a magistrate in front of a town hall. However, the Quakers' main argument for female preaching was not the glorification of weak and pious femininity; it was the assertion that, as all Quakers in the light had transcended their carnal selves, a woman preaching in public had actually transcended her womanhood.

Self-annihilation was, of course, a prerequisite for the preaching of both sexes. Richard Farnworth, an eminent Quaker leader, wrote, "I am as A white Paper Book without any line or sentence but as it is Revealed and written by ye Spirit ye Revealer of secrets."[44] But far more often than not, both men and women depicted this self-annihilation as killing the woman within the self. "Oh! come out of Words," wrote Edward Burrough,

Let . . . [the Word] dwell richly in you, which will cut down, and wholly root out the whorish Wo-man within your selves, which is not permitted to speak in the Church, . . . O that's the Clamberer, the Thief, and the Robber . . . from which the Wo-man, the unprofitable talker, the vain babbler, boasts. . . . O Male and Female-man, wherefore keep thine to within, in *thy Head,* and *the Head* of every man is *Christ Jesus:*"[45]

Both the "Male and Female-man" must die in order for the soul to live, but the "Female-man" is clearly the most essential casualty.

The degree to which Quaker women disengaged their carnal, gendered selves from their personae as prophets can be seen by the use they made of feminine images in defense of women's spiritual authority. Some women did cite biblical female prophets like Deborah or Miriam as a justification for women's public acts, but more often, "Womanhood" was used metaphorically to identify those who could *not* preach. Priscilla Cotton, a southern writer whose works included many feminine images, also argued that without God all men are reduced to being women:

Now the woman or weakness, that is man, which is his best estate or greatest wisdom is altogether vanity, that must be covered with the covering of the Spirit . . . that its nakedness may not appear. . . . Here mayst thou see . . . that the woman or weakness whether male or female, is forbidden to speak in the Church; . . . *Indeed you yourselves are the women, that are forbidden to speak in the church, that are become women.*[46]

Elizabeth Hooton, the first Quaker woman preacher and a venerated "mother in Israel" within the movement, admonished King Charles II, "Oh that thou would not give thy kingdom to your papists nor thy strength to women."[47]

From the Quakers' own perspective, their altering of the popular meaning of Womanhood, holding to it as a negative abstraction while rejecting its descriptive value for individual, sanctified women, must have seemed a very effective argument—indeed, the only possible argument, both theologically and strategically—that could justify the public authority of female prophets in a patriarchal world. This seems the only way to view Richard Hubberthorn's tract in defense of Elizabeth Leavens and Elizabeth Fletcher, which had as its subtitle, "the lewdness of those two great Mothers discovered, who have brought forth so many Children, and never had Husband." The "Mothers" were the two male justices who had persecuted the ministers, while the real women were referred to only as "two servants of the Lord."[48] It must also be said that Quakers shared prevalent assumptions about the unsuitability of women for positions of political authority; that is, authority in the world, in the body. As George Keith explained it, in a tract defending women's preaching,

It is permitted unto Men, at times, to speak in the church . . . An unlearned man may be permitted to ask a question in the church, which is not permitted unto a Woman, nor is it needful, for She may ask her Husband at home. But if the Spirit of the Lord Command or move a godly and Spiritually Learned Woman to speak, in that case she is the Lord's more than her Husband's, and she is to speak, yea, though the Husband should forbid her.[49]

Whatever the intentions of these Quaker writers, the effect of their theology must have been to impose on women, particularly southern women, a greater distance between their sense of themselves as people and as prophets, and to force them to demonstrate over and over again their essential absence from a scene they outwardly appeared to dominate. In short, the self-transcendence of Quaker men was different from the self-alienation of Quaker women: the public authority of the male Quaker was at least analogous to, if not derived from, his own gendered individuality; the authority of the woman was grounded in her total rejection of self.

This theological principle was one chief reason why southern women, who were more outwardly emotional, more concerned about self-expression and more deeply inspired by feminine spiritual images, were less active as preachers than women from the north; indeed, the great majority of those who preached only once or twice, and to local audiences, were from the south. For a woman to engage with confidence in such an unfamiliar public confrontation, one that subjected her to far more punishment than praise, she had to experience her prophetic voice as loud enough and clear enough to obliterate the voice of her own gendered self. It is in this context, rather than that of self-expression, emotional catharsis, or neurotic masochism, that we should view the energy and persistence of Elizabeth Hooton's challenge to the magistrates of New England, the seeming compulsion with which she kept on baring her back to the whip.

The different implications of Quaker theology for the preaching of men and women may help to explain why women's public language and behavior was, overall, considerably less idiosyncratic and pretentious than that of men. Women did not pile image upon image with the energy of Edward Burrough:

Howl, howl, shriek, yell and roar, ye Lustful, Cursing, Swearing, Drunken, Lewd, Superstitious, Devilish, Sensual, *Earthly Inhabitants* of the whole Earth; Bow, bow ye most surly Trees, and lofty Oaks, ye tall Cedars, and low Shrubs, *Cry out aloud;* hear, hear ye proud Waves, and boistrous

Seas, also listen ye uncircumcised, stiff-necked, and mad-raging *Bubbles,* who even hate to be reformed.[50]

Nor did women skirt the boundaries of coherent discourse as closely as did George Fox writing on the powers of the earth: "Oh Hypocrisy It makes me sick to think of them. . . . There is an ugly a slobbering hound an ugly hound an ugly slobbering hound but the Lord forgive them—destruction—destruction."[51]

A few women, fifteen to be exact, *were* chided for unruly behavior by Quaker leaders during the movement's first fifteen years, most of them from the south of England. Martha Simmonds was judged to speak in her will when she disrupted a meeting, and was accused of "seducing" James Nayler into heretical behavior. Jane Holmes "did kick against exhortation." So did Mildred Crouch, when she reputedly said that she was above the apostles.[52] The behavior of these delinquent women may have been self-centered or hysterical; it was also less bizarre than that of Thomas Holme, who lay on the floor of his prison singing at midnight, or Solomon Eccles, who climbed into a pulpit and sat sewing before the congregation and who appeared in the doorway of a church with a pan of coals on his head, or Richard Sale, who threw weeds and flowers on his own head, or Francis Howgill, who attempted to cure a crippled child by touch, or James Nayler, who rode into the city of Bristol on an ass in imitation of Jesus's entry into Jerusalem.[53] Quaker men also appeared naked in public far more often than Quaker women.[54] Of course men's symbolic behavior was derived from biblical exemplars, as was that of women, but the exemplars were chosen differently, and from a broader range. Quaker women did not climb into pulpits.

The suggestion that Quaker worship and preaching may have been more liberating or cathartic for men than for women is supported by other, indirect evidence. There is no question that both women and men experienced a sense of release and empowerment during their moments of visionary insight. On the other hand, there is little evidence of any kind to indicate that Quaker women converted because they wanted to be free of their families or to act like men, like young women dressing up as soldiers in order to find adventure and see the world. While Quaker women's conversion was often accompanied by an intense spiritual struggle and personal sacrifice, it did not represent a rejection of a whole previous way of life; the convincement of Elizabeth Hooton and Margaret Fell did not cause them to change their work, their houses, or their husbands. Indeed, most women were either married to Quakers and were converted together with their husbands and servants, or they married Quaker men after their conversion.[55] Even though they and their husbands preached independently, they corresponded with each other; women also traveled with their older children.[56]

Male Quakers, on the other hand, were often younger brothers without family advantages; most often they were the only members of families to join the movement, and they adopted Quaker plain manners as a challenge to the status hierarchy within their own households.[57] Several men renounced their families after their conversion to the movement, and this fact was dramatized in their writings, where honor and pride were contrasted with salvation as a reversal of status. Francis Howgill's testimony to his friend Edward Burrough emphasized the trauma of Burrough's conversion—cast out into the street by hardhearted parents—and his subsequent ecstatic fusion with the group; "his nearest Relations, even his own Parents cast him off as an Alien, and turned him out from their House, as not to have any part or portion therein as a son, nay, not so much as a hired servant, which this young man bore very patiently."[58] In a similar vein, James Nayler wrote that his spiritual impulse impelled him to simply walk away from his village, leaving his wife and children permanently, without his knowing why and without a word to anyone.[59] This is not to say that Quaker men were indifferent to their families' needs; Nayler, for one, continued to provide for his family and was undoubtedly gratified when his wife visited him in prison. The point is rather that male conversion was portrayed as a solitary quest, and an overturning of one's outward life, to a far greater degree than that of women.

Men may also have experienced Quaker worship as a more intense emotional release than women did, for there was a greater contrast between conventional norms of masculine behavior and the highly physical and lyrical style of Quaker worship. The great majority of the Quakers' private letters, describing their ecstacy as brides of Christ or infants nurtured by God, as well as personal anguish and uncertainty, were written by men; even allowing for the fact that men outnumbered women and were more fully liter-ate, there is no doubt of the emotional catharsis they experienced as they abandoned themselves within the collective authority and succour of the Quaker community. Of course, women also af-firmed that they were infants, cradled in the arms of God. How-ever, for a woman to affirm her own spiritual babyhood, or to express her adoration of Margaret Fell as a spiritual mother, im-plied a less dramatic reversal of status and a less radical emotional shift than it did for a man, not least because all babies and young children were commonly dressed as girls.

Mothers in Israel

Despite their infantile and apocalyptic imagery and the antisocial appearance of their quaking and prophesying, the Quakers' ulti-mate ambition was not to live in a spiritual utopia free from worldly concerns; it was to imbue worldly concerns with the inten-sity and moral stature of an exalted spiritual life. Ideally, Quaker friendships, business, and family relationships were to be liberated from egoistic striving and suffused with godly simplicity, while the communication of spiritual ecstasy was to be colored and given tangible shape by demonstrations of concrete human love and jus-tice. The new age to come would be brought about by visionary preaching—and by giving fair weight in the marketplace.

The fact that ecstatic preaching was a transient experience of mind and soul, and not a permanent office or life-style, meant that Quakers had to integrate moments of being "in the power" with other aspects of their social and personal existence; in order to be a good Quaker, one had to live on more than one level, as John Camm and John Audland did when they wrote to friends:

You are clothed with beauty and you grow in a pleasant place [and] the hand of the Lord is with you. . . . Tell [widow Alcoke] that . . . the woman saith she will pay her when she is able. She confesseth she owe her about ten pounds. . . . Remember me to the woman which heard the voice, that she must leave her country.[60]

Now it may have been a simple enough matter to synthesize ecstatic and mundane modes of expression in a private letter or in a single gesture (as when the sheriff of Nottingham, obeying a sudden impulse to preach in the streets, rushed out of the house in his slippers).[61] But how, in actual daily life, were Quakers to sustain the integration of ecstatic prayer with keeping a budget, itinerant preaching with caring for children and the necessities of business, the transcendence of all carnal needs with the needs and obligations of marriage?

The private letters of several missionaries expressed a conscious and often tortuous struggle to fulfill both mundane and spiritual obligations. In 1660, Joseph Nicholson wrote a letter to Margaret Fell at Swarthmore, telling her that his wife was in labor and that some Quaker extremists refused to associate with them because they were clearly not celibate.[62] The following year, writing from Dover, he discussed his and his wife's plans in a long, depressed letter to Fell. He himself was going back to Virginia,

but which way Jane will go or how its with her as to that I can not much say how it will be with her, . . . if there lie any thing upon Jane to go into the country she may use her liberty. . . .it seems to me [right] for her to leave the child if she could be sent into the north to the rest of our children. . . . My trouble hath been great many times since I went from this nation. . . . I am much short of what hath been or may be required of me.[63]

Given the practical and emotional difficulties of early Quaker life, both in and out of the body, one is struck by the extent to which leading Quaker women succeeded in combining ecstatic prayer and public evangelizing with the more conventional activities of child rearing, charity work, caring for Quakers in prison, petitioning Parliament, and negotiating with magistrates. Margaret Fell preached at meetings; she wrote treatises, polemics, formal epistles, and private letters; she organized the itineraries of missionaries; she received and offered spiritual counseling; she acted as a clearinghouse for Quaker correspondence between two continents and advised Quakers on the publication of their writings; she also made sure that traveling Quakers had shoes. Elizabeth Hooton was active buying and selling property, distributing charity, and advocating prison reform, during the same period that she was admonishing the English king and the magistrates of Boston, and (aged at least sixty) was stripped to the waist, tied to a cart, and whipped out of town and into the wilderness at least three different times because she kept coming back to preach. This integration of visionary ecstacy with more ordinary behavior was often sustained on an almost daily basis; some prophets made missionary journeys lasting months before returning home to their families, but in many other cases, they preached in the streets or at meetings for worship and then came home, nursed their babies, and served supper.

The name for this archetypal female Quaker was the "mother in Israel." It was in the persona of Margaret Fell, and in that of Elizabeth Hooton, Ann Downer, Rebecca Travers, Margaret Newby and many others, that the Quakers' ability to integrate pragmatism and spirituality was most fully expressed; and it was these women who made the transition between ecstacy and sanctified daily life at least a partial reality for other Friends, male and female. As Joseph Nicholson struggled to reconcile the dissonant modes of his existence as father, husband, and minister, he turned to Margaret Fell as a practical and symbolic parent, both to the movement and to him personally:

I was not free to write so much to [my wife] about the child but I have somewhat hinted at it in her letter which she will et thee see. . . . I was free to let thee know what I think in it. . . . God almighty be with thee and thine who hath been and art famous above the rest of families upon earth . . . which makes many love both thee and them because of thy anointing. . . . The lord god order thee for thou hast ordered many aright.[64]

Not surprisingly, and regardless of the Quakers' democratic values, Quaker mothers in Israel also tended to be those with some money, property, and a relatively privileged class position; those women whose position had always accustomed them to deference, and who also had the skills to manage both magistrates and Friends.[65] The Quakers' reputation for financial integrity and honesty in business was also largely due to the influence of these prominent women, particularly Margaret Fell, who led in establishing and administering a fund collected at Kendal "for the service of truth," beginning already in 1654, before the distribution of funds was regularized by George Fox in women's meetings.

The fact that women's conversion to Quakerism was less disruptive than men's and their position as ministers less authoritative, may account for their greater success in integrating ecstatic and mundane modes of existence in the years following their convincement. Individual Quaker men were, of course, equally successful in this regard, just as individual women were successful as theological writers and preachers; but men tended to present themselves not as "fathers in Israel," but as zealots wholly given to preaching as a vocation. Edward Burrough was thus described by his best friend: "He made the Work of the Lord [i.e., preaching] his whole business, without taking so much liberty unto himself or about any outward occasion in this World, as to spend one Week to himself . . . these ten years."[66] Conversely, women, as mothers in Israel, continued and greatly amplified their customary roles; for the figure of the mother in Israel as a nurturer, provider, and overseer of many children, was a traditional one for seventeenth-century women. Widows, schoolteachers, and women as deputy husbands had this kind of autonomy, but in early Quakerism it was not an ad hoc measure—taking over in the absence of male authority—but a positive precept of the movement. Indeed, the Quakers' conception of womanly virtue went far beyond the persona of the virtuous goodwife, and this at a time when misogynist attitudes proliferated to a degree unheard of fifty years earlier. The figure of the mother in Israel was also unique among radical religious groups in early modern England; certainly the relationship of these women to eminent male Quakers was not comparable to that of, say, Muggletonian women with their male messianic and paternalist leader, or of Baptist women with the ministers who recorded and categorized their experiences of convincement.[67] Thus do the facts belie the stereotypes. Our image of the hysterial female visionary in early Quaker history has more to do with expectations of female behavior than it does with objective reality; far from being excessively undisciplined, extremist, or hysterical, women's predominant role in early Quakerism was to hold the movement together.

The Quakers claimed that they had attained the perfection of Eden. In a sense they *were* in Eden, for the looser atmosphere of the Civil War gave them space to attempt new modes of worship and behavior, before their apocalyptic hopes were disappointed and before increased persecution forced them to recast their public posture in a more conventional mode. It also allowed them to ignore the contradictions implicit in their theology of class and gender relationships. For while Quakers maintained that men and women in the light were equal and outside the law—including the law of patriarchy—they were no less convinced that Friends' service "in the light" must be conducted "in their measure" as obedient servants, nurturing mothers, and authoritative heads of families.

Nevertheless, what the Quakers experienced in the early years of the movement cannot be dismissed as a liminal movement of hysterics or lotus-eaters; rather, it was a quite conscious and frequently successful struggle to integrate disparate modes of being, times of being "in the power"—travelling, writing, prophesying, and ecstatic suffering—with other, much longer periods of mundane existence. This most characteristic element of early Quakerism could not have evolved as it did, nor could it have been sustained in the concrete lives of early and later Friends, without the readiness of Quaker men to exhibit traditionally feminine and childlike behavior, and without Quaker women's willingness and capacity to take on the activist and leadership dimensions of comradeship and parenthood. In their weakest moments, the Quakers' struggle to achieve this integration was clumsy and painful; but in their finest moments, Quaker women and men were able to balance states of spiritual ecstacy and self-annihilation with a concern for the practical, ethical, and affective elements of everyday life. This integration of spiritual intensity, moral integrity, and attentiveness to the human needs of Friends was expressed with great power in a single sentence by the prophet Margaret Newby, a stout, comfortable, well-to-do matron with several children, who preached and was martyred in 1657: "A friend did hold me in her arms, the power of the Lord was so strong in me, and I cleared my conscience, and I was moved to sing."[68]

NOTES

1. Letter, N.d., Friends House, London, Port. Mss. iii, 3, 10,; quoted in Emily Manners, *Elizabeth Hooton: First Quaker Woman Preacher (1600–1672)* (London: Headley Bros., 1911), 10, 38.

2. Letter of Elizabeth Hooton to Friends, London, 17 October 1662; quoted in Manners, *Elizabeth Hooton,* 36–37.

3. "Lamentation for Bosston and Camberig Her Sister," Friends, Port. Mss. iii, 36; quoted in Manners, *Elizabeth Hooton, 51.*

4. Friends, Port. Mss. iii, 73; quoted in Manners, *Elizabeth Hooton,* 60. Her arrest in Massachusetts followed her attempt to purchase a house and burial ground for the use of Quakers.

5. Testimony of James Lancaster, quoted in Manners, *Elizabeth Hooton,* 73.

6. I have counted 253 preachers and writers from 1650 to 1660, chiefly using the Great Book of Sufferings (Mss. Friends House, London) and the Dictionary of Quaker Biography (Mss. Friends House and Haverford College Quaker Collection).

7. On women missionaries, see Rufus Jones, *The Quakers in the American Colonies* (London: Macmillan, 1911), 26ff, and Mabel Brailsford, *Quaker Women, 1650–1690* (London: Duckworth, 1915). On Ireland: Brailsford, 179. On America: William C. Braithwaite, *The Beginnings of Quakerism,* 2nd ed. (Cambridge: Cambridge University Press, 1955), 402. Twelve of the twenty-two missionaries to Massachusetts before 1660 were women. (Hugh Barbour, "Quaker Prophetesses and Mothers in Israel," in J. William Frost and John M. Moore, eds., *Seeking the Light: Essays in Quaker History in Honor of Edwin B. Bronner* [Wallingford, Pa.: Pendle Hill Publications, and Haverford, Pa.: Friends Historical Association, 1986], 44.) On Elizabeth Harris: Kenneth L. Carroll, "Elizabeth Harris, the Founder of American Quakerism," *Quaker History* 57:2 (Autumn 1968): 96–98. On Mary Fell: George Fox, *Journal* 1656, quoted in Lucy V. Hodgkin, *A Quaker Saint of Cornwall: Loveday Hambly and her Guests* (London: Longmans Green 1927), 101–102. On Hooton: Friends, Port. Mss. iii, 57, quoted in Brailsford, 36.

On Quaker children prophesying in America, see Lyle Koehler, *A Search for Power: The "Weaker Sex" in Seventeenth-Century New England* (Urbana: University of Illinois Press, 1980), 303. Hannah Wright was imprisoned at age thirteen for preaching in Boston. Patience Scott preached at eleven or twelve (James Bowden, *The History of the Society of Friends in America,* 2 vols. [London: C. Gilpin, 1850], I, 168–169). Elizabeth Fletcher was flogged in the marketplace at Oxford when she was fifteen, and would die of exposure and ill treatment before she was twenty. The ages of few of the women prophets are given with precision; most seem to have been married adults in their twenties or thirties.

8. For an early example of this behavior, see *The Saints Testimony Finishing through Sufferings: or, The Proceedings of the Court against the Servants of Jesus . . . held in Banbury in the County of Oxon, the 26 day of the seventh Moneth, 1655* (London: For Giles Calvert, 1655).

9. Nigel Smith distinguishes between a prophet like Eleanor Davies and the radicals, including Quakers: "The difference . . . is that while she is concerned with the interpretation of divinely inscribed knowledge, the radicals are concerned with the nature of the inspiration itself, either as 'experience' or prophecy, so turning entirely from knowledge to power, from a concern for comprehending God's intentions for mankind to a concern for God working in the self." ("The Interior Word: Aspects of the Use of Language and Rhetoric in Radical Puritan and Sectarian Literature, c.1640– c.1660," Oxford, D.Phil. diss., 1985, 209).

10. Ronald Knox, *Enthusiasm: A Chapter in the History of Religion, with Special Reference to the XVII and XVIII Centuries* (Oxford: Oxford University Press, 1950).

11. David S. Lovejoy, *Religious Enthusiasm in the New World: Heresy to Revolution* (Cambridge: Harvard University Press, 1985), 68; Braithwaite, *Beginnings;* Christopher Hill, *The World Turned Upside Down: Radical Ideas during the English Revolution* (New

York: Viking Press, 1972), chaps 3, "The Island of Great Bedlam," and 15, "Base Impudent Kisses."

12. Brailsford, *Quaker Women,* 222–225.

13. Jane Wither's testimony, in James Nayler, *A Discovery of the Man of Sin* (London, 1656) 45, quoted in Barbour, *The Quakers in Puritan England* (New Haven: Yale University Press, 1964), 117–118.

14. Margaret Killam to George Fox, about 1653, Swarthmore Mss., transcript II, 667. Friends.

15. Katherine Evans and Sarah Cheevers, *This is a Short Relation of Some of the Cruel Sufferings (for the Truths Sake) of Katherine Evans & Sarah Chevers, in the Inquisition in the Isle of Malta* (London: For Robert Wilson, 1662), 12–13.

16. Judith Boulbie, "A Few Words as a Warning from the Lord to the inhabitants of Londonderry, and also to the whole Nation of Ireland," 1679, quoted in Thomas Wight and John Rutty, *A History of the Rise and Progress of the People Called Quakers in Ireland* (Dublin: I. Jackson, 1751), 142–144.

17. On the meaning of signs—tearing clothes, going naked, breaking pottery, and so on—see Kenneth L. Carroll, "Early Quakers and 'Going Naked as a Sign' " *Quaker History,* 67:2 (Autumn 1978): 69–87.

18. Elizabeth Hendricks, "An Epistle to Friends in England, To be Read in their Assemblies in the Fear of the Lord" (London: N.p., 1672).

19. Mary Howgill, "A Remarkable Letter of Mary Howgill to Oliver Cromwell, called Protector" (London: N.p., 1657), 1.

20. Christopher Story, *Life,* quoted in Luella Wright, *The Literary Life of the Early Friends, 1650–1725* (New York: Columbia University Press, 1932), 228.

21. Brailsford, *Quaker Women,* 237.

22. Edward Burrough, "A Warning from the Lord to the Inhabitants of Underbarrow, and so to all the Inhabitants in England" (London: For Giles Calvert, 1654) 32–35.

23. James Nayler defended the Quakers' trembling by saying that it isn't the body they really abhor; it is ego. ("An Answer to 28 Queries Sent Out by Francis Harris to those People He Calls Quakers," London: For Giles Calvert, 1655, 21–22).

24. On manners, see Norbert Elias, *The History of Manners,* vol. 1, *The Civilizing Process,* trans. Edmund Jephcott (New York: Pantheon Books, 1982). On the rituals of family, marriage, and popular culture, see Lawrence Stone, *The Family, Sex and Marriage in England 1500–1800* (London: Harper & Row, 1977).

25. Richard Hubberthorn to George Fox, Norwich Castle Prison, 13/9th month (Nov.), 1654, Swarthmore Mss. iv, 235 (transcript II, 567–568).

26. John Audland to Margaret Fell, Swanington, 1656, Swarthmore Mss. i, 7.

27. *Journal,* vol. 1, 39, quoted in Gadt, "Women and Protestant Culture: The Quaker Dissent from Puritanism" (Ph.D. diss., U.C.L.A., 1974), 185.

28. Thomas Aldam to George Fox, N.d., Swarthmore Mss. iii, 39.

29. Quoted in Barbour, *Quakers in Puritan England,* 132–133.

30. John Perrot to Quakers from Lyons, c. 1661, quoted in William C. Braithwaite, *The Second Period of Quakerism,* 2d ed. (Cambridge: Cambridge University Press, 1961), 231–232.

31. The acts of writing and public prophecy were actually more similar than one might suppose; writing involved public confrontation as well, since works were hawked by their authors on street corners or in front of taverns, or handed to magistrates like a

modern summons. Conversely, acts of preaching were later revised for publication, as were some private letters and epistles to Friends.

32. Mary Howgill to Margaret Fell, n.d., Swarthmore Mss., i, 378 (transcript II, 493).

33. Mary Howgill, "A Remarkable Letter of Mary Howgill to Oliver Cromwell, called Protector," (London: N.p., 1657), 4–6.

34. On men dressing as women, see Natalie Z. Davis, *Society and Culture in Early Modern France* (Stanford: Stanford University Press, 1975), 124–152.

35. "An Account of the Birth, Education and Sufferings for the Truth's Sake of that Faithful Friend Elizabeth Andrews," *Journal of the Friends Historical Society* 26 (1929): 3–8.

36. On Fell's relationship to her first husband, see Bonnelyn Young Kunze, "The Family, Social and Religious Life of Margaret Fell," (Ph.D. diss., U. of Rochester, 1986) 37–39. She contrasts the experience of Margaret Fell with that of another gentry family, that of Ralph Verney, where the wife and children were beholden to the steward, who exercised authority in the father's absences. Margaret Fell, and later her children, had responsibility for their estate in the absence of their mother. (Kunze, 50–51). Each Fell sister had her own expense account, and Susanna, for one, was able to lend large sums of money (Kunze, 58). On the social status of male Quakers, see Richard T. Vann, *The Social Development of English Quakerism, 1655–1755* (Cambridge: Harvard University Press, 1969), 97–98; most prominent male ministers in Norfolk and Buckinghamshire were prosperous yoemen, wholesale traders, professionals, or gentlemen.

37. Margaret Killam, "A Warning from the Lord to the Teachers and People of Plimouth" (London: For Giles Calvert, 1656), 2.

38. Dorothy White, "An Epistle of Love, and of Consolation unto Israel (London, 1661), 1–9.

39. Elizabeth Adams to George Fox, Whitfield, 26/3/57. Swarthmore Mss. iv, 37 (transcript IV,9).

40. The most effusive examples of hero worship came from letters by southern women, for example, that to James Nayler by Hannah Stranger: "Oh thou fairest of ten thousand, thou only begotten son of God, how myheart panteth after thee." (Ralph Farmer, *Sathan Enthron'd in his Chair of Pestilence, or Quakerism in its exaltation,* London: For Edward Thomas, 1657, 7–8. The letter was also signed by John Stranger). On Quaker women in trouble with Friends, see below, n.52. Of sixteen in trouble, nine were from south and seven from north, but the trouble was more serious with women from the south.

41. On the atmosphere of the northern counties, see Barbour, *The Quakers in Puritan England,* 43–44, 72–84. Margaret Killam, Elizabeth Hooton, Dorothy and Mabel Camm, Mary Aldam, Mary Howgill, Ann Audland, and Ann Blaykling all belonged to Seeker or Bible study groups.

42. Dorothea Scott Gotherson was actually related to Anne Hutchinson and Hutchinson's sister Katherine Scott, another Quaker minister. (Katherine Scott to John Winthrop, 17, 4th mo., 1658, quoted in G. D. Scull, *Dorothea Scott, Otherwise Gotherson & Hogben, of Egerton House, Kent, 1611–1680.* [Oxford: Parker & Co., 1883], 33–35.) Mary Dyer was a close friend of Hutchinson's before her convincement to Quakerism, (Bowden, *Friends in America,* 163ff). Sarah Bennett and Mary Prince mentioned the prophet Anna Trapnel in a letter to George Fox in 1656 (Swarthmore Mss. I, 163). Many women described going from sect to sect before their convincement, for instance Mary Penington and Martha Simmonds. Barbour notes that southern Quakers had more diverse backgrounds than those from the north, including tailors, shoemakers, carpen-

ters; of the women, many were domestic servants. (Barbour, *The Quakers in Puritan England*, 92).

43. On the biblical tradition that the last shall be first, see Rosalie Colie, *Paradoxia Epidemica: The Renaissance Tradition of Paradox* (Princeton: Princeton University Press, 1966), 24–38. On the paradox of strength in weakness applied to women, see Ian Maclean, *Woman Triumphant: Feminism in French Literature 1610–1652* (Oxford: Oxford University Press, 1977), 21–22.

44. Richard Farnworth to George Fox and Margaret Fell, November 12, 1654, Swarthmore Mss., iii, 50, iii, 51 (transcript II, 61)

45. Edward Burrough, "An Alarm to all Flesh. . ." (London: For Robert Wilson, 1660)," 7–8. See also the argument by Richard Farnworth in his tract, "A Woman Forbidden to Speak in the Church," 3–4: "The Woman or wisdom of the Flesh is forbidden to speak in the Church, that is, of the things of God, for that which is flesh is flesh. . . . It is the Man child *Christ Jesus*, . . . that is to declare the Fathers will, and that is permitted to speak."

46. Priscilla Cotton and Mary Cole, "To the Priests and People of England, We Discharge our Consciences, and Give Them Warning" (London: For Giles Calvert, 1655), 7–8.

47. "El. Hooton to some Spirits who were gone out from ye truth," Friends, Port. Mss. iii, 33, 13 6th month, 1667, quoted in Manners, *Elizabeth Hooton*, 57.

48. Richard Hubberthorn, "A true testimony of the zeal of Oxford-Professors," *A Collection of the Several Books and Writings of that Faithful Servant of God Richard Hubberthorn.* . . (London: Printed for William Warwick, 1663), 41–42.

49. George Keith, *The Woman Preacher of Samaria* (London: N.p., 1674), 11.

50. Edward Burrough, "An Alarm to all Flesh. . . ," 1.

51. George Fox, *Cambridge Journal*, II, 172, quoted in Barbour, *The Quakers in Puritan England*, 137.

52. Martha Simmonds, Hannah Stranger, and Dorcas Erbury were involved in the Nayler episode. Jane Holmes was involved in an argument over the distribution of funds among prisoners; she was also ducked as a scold for preaching in the streets at Malton (Thomas Aldam to Friends, 1653, Swarthmore Mss. iii, 40; see also Braithwaite, *Beginnings*, 72). Katherine Crooke was reported to have been "hasty and rash" by saying in a public debate that she would have known God even without Scripture (Edward Bourne to G. F., Hereford prison, June–July 1664, Swarthmore Mss. iv, 52). Mary Howgill was "distracted" (Barbour, *The Quakers in Puritan England*, 121). Mildred Crouch and "Judy" disrupted meetings after the Nailer episode. Elizabeth Williams and Thomas Castley were ruled out of order when preaching (A.R.B. Mss., Friends, Transcript 61, Edward Burrough to George Fox, 5 July 1654). Elizabeth Morgan "bred dissension" (Braithwaite, 388 and n.10). Mary Clark was "ensnared" by Dorothy Waugh. Ann Blaykling was "out of unity"; she gathered a party to work on Sundays and not pay taxes, but pay tithes, (Braithwaite, 345–346). Agnes Wilkinson was sent home to Margaret Fell for acting "contrary to ye light, in filthiness," and with a guardian (Thomas Aldam to Margaret Fell, 1654, Swarthmore Mss. iv, 89, and Barbour, 104,121). Gervase Benson wrote to Margaret Fell, "As for my wife she is come more of late into moderation in words: And surely the forwardness of some that came to her, in Judging her who them did comprehend and their Judgment did hurt and no good at all: but rather gave the deceipt advantage" (Swarthmore Mss. iv, 230). Isabel Garnet, a widow was "exalted," along with Thomas Wilson, by some "rebellious Quakers at Grayrigg (John Camm to Margaret Fell, Camsgill, Preston Patrick, June, 1655, Swarthmore Mss. ii,

339). Other women, not ministers, were referred to as having "a high spirit" (Mrs. Bennet, Geoffrey Nuttall, *Early Quaker Letters* [London: The Library, Friends House, 1952], #283, 1656), "deceit strong in her" (wife of William Hall, *EQL* #175, 1655), "wrought on" (wife of Captain Thomas Siddall, *EQL* #6, 1652); Agnes Ayrey was condemned for fornication with Christopher Atkinson (Barbour, 121). We don't know, of course, what terms like "out of order" actually meant, or whether they meant different things for men and women; John Camm, who judged Isabel Garnet, maintained that Quakers "were pretty subjected under me before [Wilson] came." Several men were, of course, also judged for excessive behavior, including the leader Richard Hubberthorn (Hubberthorn to Margaret Fell c. 1653, quoted in Barbour, 121).

53. On Holme, his letter to Margaret Fell from Chester prison c. 1653 (Swarthmore Mss., 329). On Sale, letter of Sale to George Fox, 28, 8th month 1855 (Swarthmore Mss). On Eccles, see Solomon Eccles, "In the yeare 59," (London: Printed for M.W., 1659), 1–7. On Burrough and Howgill's unsuccessful attempt to cure a sick boy, see Fox's *Book of Miracles,* edited by Henry J. Cadbury (New York: Octagon Books, 1973), 12. Hugh Barbour notes that "No women Friends felt . . . [the burden to go naked as a sign] as regularly as did William Simpson, Richard Robinson, Samuel Cater . . . and Solomon Eccles; two Massachusetts women Friends along with three Englishwomen did so once." ("Quaker Prophetesses," 47). See also Kenneth Carroll, "Early Quakers and 'Going Naked'. . . ."

54. "Early Quakers and 'Going Naked'. . . ."

55. Brailsford, *Quaker Women,* 158–159. Families who converted together: William and Anne Dewsbury, Ann Blaykling and her brother John, John and Ann Leake, Richard and Elizabeth Tomlinson, Gervase Benson and his wife Dorothy, John and Ann Audland (she preached with her husband, whom she had met in a separatist congregation where he preached), their friends John and Mabel Camm, and the Camm's servants, Jane and Dorothy Waugh, Dorothea Gotherson and her husband, Mary Howgill and her brother Francis, and Margaret Killam and her brother Thomas (who was married to the preacher Mary Aldam), sister Joan, and husband John. See Hugh Barbour and Arthur O. Roberts, eds., *Early Quaker Writings 1650–1700* (Grand Rapids: Eerdmans, 1973), 58; Scull, *Dorothea Scott,* 6; I. Ross, *Margaret Fell,* 48; John Camm and John Audland, "The Memory of the Righteous Revived" (London: Andrew Sowle, 1689). Mary Pease, Mary Askew and Anne Clayton were unmarried servants but members of the extended family at Swarthmore; Mary Pease wrote to Fell of her "sisters" Bridget and Sarah, and signed her letter, "thy Daughter" (Kunze, "*Margaret Fell,*" 82). Elizabeth Hooton's husband and children converted on her example. Grace Barwick, Sarah Cheevers, Ann Downer Whitehead, Elizabeth Leavens, and Katherine Evans were married to Quakers. Dorcas Erbury was the daughter of a Quaker. Ann Austin and Mary Clark were married when they left for America. Elizabeth Fletcher and Elizabeth Smith were unmarried. Barbara Blaugdone was a widow and loner, but even she went to her relations in Cork, Ireland, to preach. No information was available on Sarah Blackborow, Sarah Gibbons, Anne Gould, Mary Prince, Joan Vokins(?), Mary Weatherhead, and Anne Wilson (see Barbour, "Prophetesses"). Margaret Fell and Mary Dyer were supported by their husbands who were not Friends.

56. The Swarthmore manuscripts contain numerous letters between wives and husbands who preached separately. After Camm and Audland visited Banbury in 1654, their wives carried on their work there (Braithwaite, *Beginnings,* 199). Fell and Hooton traveled with their daughters. Patience Scott traveled to Boston with her mother. (Koeh-

ler, *Search for Power,* 303). John and Mabel Camm wrote together to Margaret Fell, describing his back injury and their desire to visit Fell.

57. Vann, *English Quakerism,* 85, 174–175.

58. Francis Howgill, "A Testimony Concerning the Life, Death, Trials, Travels and Labours of Edward Burrough," (London: William Warwick, 1662), 7.

59. William Dewsbury also left wife and children to preach. George Fox hardly saw his family after he became a minister. Fox's letter to his parents, written probably in 1652, is quoted in *EQL* 486; the editors note Fox's "need to establish the authority of his own inner voice over against his father's judgment." Also see Vann, *English Quakerism,* 175; Vann maintains that the "great majority" of converts in Norfolk and Buckinghamshire were the only ones of families to join.

60. Audland and Camm to E. Burrough and F. Howgill, 9 Sept. 1654, A.R.B. Mss. 1–2, 183.

61. On the sherrif of Nottingham, see George Fox, *Journal* (London: Religious Society of Friends, 1975), 41.

62. A group of Quakers, mainly in America, advocated total celibacy, (Braithwaite *Beginnings,* 236; *EQW* 520, 536).

63. Nicholson to M. F., Dover Castle 20 April 1661. Swarthmore Mss. II, 939–940.

64. Ibid.

65. The largest meetings of Friends were frequently held in the houses of well-to-do widows like Loveday Hambly of Cornwall. On Hambly, see Hodgkin, *A Quaker Saint of Cornwall.* Kunze draws a parallel between the roles of Margaret Fell and, later, William Penn, as figures whose higher class position gave them added authority as stabilizers of the movement.

66. Francis Howgill's Testimony to Edward Burrough, 9.

67. The Baptists John Rogers and Henry Walker had great influence over their communities. (Smith, "Interior word," 219). On the Muggletonians see, as one example among many, the letter of Lodowijk Muggleton to Mrs. Elizabeth Dickinson of Cambridge, August 28, 1658: "John Reeve and myself, the chosen Witnesses of the Spirit, we having the commission and burden of the Lord upon us, We are made the object of your faith, . . . so that you shall be perfectly whole as to the relation to the fears of eternal death . . . and your faith being in me, as the object in relation to the commission of the Spirit . . . and . . . you may be sure, I do declare you one of the blessed of the Lord to all eternity." (A. Delamaine and T. Terry, eds., *A Volume of Spiritual Epistles . . . by John Reeve and Lodowicke Muggleton* [N.p., 1755], 14–15.)

68. Norman Penney, ed., *"The First Publishers of Truth" Being Early Records . . . of the Introduction of Quakerism into the Counties of England and Wales,* (London: Headley Bros., 1907), 268–269.

DOCUMENTS

The first document is a short, undated tract by Elizabeth Hooton, "To the King and both Houses of Parliament" (1670), found in the Quaker Collection, Haverford College. Hooton wrote a great many such tracts during her career as a prophet and missionary, some of them short fragments she may have handed to a magistrate as he passed from the town hall, others more extended works she may have intended to publish. These tracts are largely in manuscript, in the Friends House Collection in London and at Haverford; many of them are excerpted in Manners's biography of Hooton. Hooton's chief concerns—the rights of ordinary citizens and the moral and social corruption of the clergy and magistrates—were typical of Quaker writing, particularly of prophets from the northern counties of England.

The second document is a private letter by John Killam, written while he was in prison in the castle of York in 1655, to Margaret Fell, a noted "mother in Israel," and copied from the Swarthmore transcript in Friends House, London. Killam was one of the "Valiant Sixty," a group of Quakers, mainly from the northern counties of Westmoreland, Lancashire and Yorkshire, who traveled south in the early 1650s to evangelize England and the world. John Killam's wife Margaret was also a minister; his sister Joan was an ardent Friend but not an active preacher.

The letter opens with a characteristically effusive passage extolling Margaret Fell in terms that are both erotic and extremely fluid; Killam's images, indeed the imagery in most of the letters addressed to Margaret Fell, are modeled on biblical language. The letter goes on to give news of his wife, who was preaching in Reading and traveling on to Plymouth to visit two other Friends who were in prison there. Typically, Friends and their wives preached separately, but corresponded with Margaret Fell and George Fox, and with each other; surviving letters between husbands and wives convey a mutual respect for each other's independent activities in the "lamb's war," as well as personal affection that was transformed, but not effaced, by religious zeal.

The letter concludes with personal greetings to individual Friends. Killam describes being in prison with nine other Quakers, including Captain Siddal's wife, his companion "above all ye Rest." Quakers in prison attempted to stay close together, continuing to hold religious meetings and, where possible, to carry on their trades. Prisoners had to pay for their own supplies, and Friends from outside regularly brought food and funds to the inmates.

The Swarthmore collection in Friends House Library (and on microfilm at Haverford and Swarthmore colleges) is a massive collection of letters and documents from the early period of Quakerism; the bulk of the letters are to Margaret Fell and George Fox. Margaret Fell was the coordinator of correspondence of Friends in England and abroad; she received and answered letters from Friends everywhere, many of them as adulatory as Killam's. One of the significant characteristics of John Killam's letter, and of the hundreds of other letters in the Swarthmore collection, is the synthesis of biblical lyricism with intimate, highly emotional expression, and with the communication of concrete events and practical detail.

This letter is reprinted here by permission of the Library Committee of the London Yearly Meeting of the Religious Society of Friends.

To the King and both Houses of Parliament

Friends, Consider in time, what you have done in City and Country by the late Act,[1] How you have ruinated hundreds of Ancient House-keepers in the Countrey, and the cry of the Innocent is entred into the Ears of the Lord against you that have done it, consider therefore what you will do with these poor people you have impoverished and restore them their goods again, for they were relievers of the poor, and payed their Rents and Taxes duly, But the Justices and some of the Priest informers bought their goods for half that they were worth, and drunkards, and swearers runs away with the rest, and they swear that men are at meetings when they are not, and by false swearing they compass mens goods into their hands, which is Theft and so these Robbers have entred upon our goods, and Men, Women and Children are by these means driven to great want, they having some few Months ago enough to relieve others, so if you consider not these things in time it will bring a Ruination both upon King and Countrey, so it is good to consider in time before it be too late, and take off this Act, and make better Laws, least you ruinate all, for all this done besides all bodily abuses, consider what they have done in this City they pull down our houses, they batter and bruise Men and Women with their Swords and Guns, with their Halberts, with their Pikes and Staves, running upon us with Horses, What may we expect but that many of them be *Papists,* and outlandish men that doth it, if such wickedness be tolerated to destroy honest people who serves the Lord with all their hearts, and great Companies that follows Mountebanks and Play houses and other rude pastimes that are upheld in this City, what may we expect but that the hand of the Lord may fall suddenly upon you, therefore in time repent and take heed and do Justice and love, mercy, and walk humbly with your God, that you may find place of Repentance, least you be shut out for ever, I am a lover of your souls who would not have you perish.

Elizabeth Hooton

[1]Most likely the second Conventicle Act passed by Parliament in February 1670.

ffrom john Killam to M:(argaret) F:(ell) 1655

Dear Sister

in thee eternall trueth of god, with whom my life is present in yt love which changeth not, nor never fades away, butt endures forever, in yt i am present with thee, which all Bonds & prisons cannot seperate, eternall praises bee to our Lord god forevermore, my deare sister this Love towards mee is greate, and over mee thou art tender as A nurseinge mother Refreshinge thie tender plant, yt itt may grow upp in ye encrease of god, truelie my deare heart, I was much: Refreshed with ye Readinge of thie Letter, And itt doth much reioyce mee to heare of thie faithfullness in ye measure of god which hee hath Comitted unto thee, thou shalt not Loose thie Reward, Happie, yea thrice happie art thou thee Cheifest amongst women thou blessed of ye Lord Oh i am Constrained & my Love towards thee cannot bee Contained, which constraines mee thus to write unto thee, my deare heart what cann I say more unto thee, All yt cann be expressed is farr short of my love yt flowes forth unto thee, my dearest Love of Loves, thie Love towards mee is answered with thee same love which flowes from mee to thee againe, which love Runs out freelie unto thee, which noe tongue cann expresse, in ye Bowells of love I doe ye Greete, where wee have unitie together, and lies downe in ye Armes of Love embraceinge each the other, in yt where wee cannot bee seperated, everlastinge praises bee unto the Lord god Almightie, who is worthie, who is god over all Blassed forever Amen. My deare heart though i bee A prisoner as in ye outward, yett my spirit is att Libertie in thee Lord which all the Powers of ye earth cannot prison, And truelie therein is my Joy & Comforte All praises bee to ye Lord god forever, who hath not onelie Called mee to beare testimony to his everlastinge trueth, but hath Counted mee worthie to suffer for his name sake And therein my exceedinge Joy &

greate Reward, and hearein I have peace which carries mee above all ye world and worldlie enioymnets, which are not worthie to bee compared, to ye grace of god which is Reveailed in mee, which is my Joy which ye whole world is Ignorant of which makes them Run on headlonge to theirr owne destruction. And though thee adversarie of god bee suffered to keepe this outward man in prison still yett I cann truelie say itt is for good. And herein is my Joy fullfilled, Joy: Joy, eternall which never fades away but endures for aye: And itt is but A little & ye Redeemed ones of ye Lord shall Returne to Sion, with songes and everlastinge Joy upon theire heads, Haleluiah to ye highest the Lords god Omnipotent Raigneth who is kinge of kings & Lord of Lords, god blessed for ever Amen . . . And as for my wife I Received A letter from her upon ye last day of ye 3d moneth 55 And shee writes she was att A place called Reedinge upon ye 27th day of ye 3d moneth 55 beinge ye first day of ye weeke, att one Called Justice Curtises att a meeteinge, And shee writes shee was to goe away ye next day towards Plimmoth where shee heard Miles Halhead & Tho: Saltehouse was in prison, My Deare Love is with thie daughters M:ff: B:ff: my Love is deare & neare unto them and to ye Rest of those litle ones ye tender plants, my little ones all in ye measure of god be faithfull in ye light dwell which Comprehends thee world and all thee darke ways thereof And ye Lord god all mightie blesse preserve & keepe you by his mightie Power to his everlastinge praise now & forever more litle Babes & Lambes of god, my deare Love is with ye Rest of thie familie whom I cannot name, who are of ye houshould of faith & faithfull in thee works of god, thee blesseinge of ye lord god be amonst you & Rest upon you, yt are faithfull in ye measure of god, made manifest to you, in ye light dwell which cuts down & Judgeth out all that which is Contrarie to ye light, yt with ye light which comes from Christ you may see your saviour yt Jesus Christ, whom to know is life eternall therefore in ye unitie & bee dilligent to ye pure of god in you my Deare and precious one my Love towards thee cannot bee expressed in words nor writeinge for truelie itt Reacheth forth unto thee not faiginge nor vanishinge but eternall & everlatinge for evermore, what cann I say more unto ye Ah my deare & precious one, thou art mine & I am thine in yt which cannot be seperated And in thie bosome I Lie downe, & finde Refreshment Read where I am upon thie hidden understand-inge, whre I cann never forgett thee, Soe fare you all well my deare hearts and thee bleseing of ye Lord god Rest upon you all in ye Bowells of love I you all greete, And as one I you all Salute with an holy Kisse, where my salutation is, . . . adeiu My deare hearts.

Remember my deare & tender love to my deare Brother Robert Widders & his wife When thou seest eithr of them my unfeigned Love is with them, both in that which can-not be separated they are my deare & precious ones, they are neare & deare & unto mee, my love to them cannot be ex-pressed in words for verelie itt flowes out freelie unto them with

your dear Brother in yᵉ eternall trueth which never fades away but endures for aye: John Killam I am even full of Love towards you & cann scarce keepe pen from paper more I write more I may

wee are tenn in prison here *Rodger Hebden* Captaine Sid-dall wife is my neare & deare Companyon in yᵉ Bonds of love shee above all yᵉ Rest, though yᵉ other in theire measures yett shee is my yoake fellow, in thee true fellowshipe of Love.

ffrom yorke Castle thee 9th day of the 4th month 1655

T W O

The Eighteenth Century

MARY MAPLES DUNN

Latest Light on Women
of Light

I WAS ASKED to sum up for this volume our understanding of
the history of Quaker women in seventeenth- and eighteenth-
century America, but I discovered that in order to undertake that
exercise I had first to ask why we are so interested in early Quaker
women. And to follow this question with another about the appro-
priateness of isolating the experience of American Quaker women
who were, after all, members of an Atlantic community of
Friends. Only then could I make some assessment of what has been
achieved in writing their history and arrive at some consideration,
in general, of three avenues of approach: biography, gender-role
study, and female experience. And finally, this led me to try to
suggest what still might be done. The debt everywhere to contemporary writing in social history will be obvious.

To begin with the first of my questions, why should we take an
interest in Quaker women? I can give you a text, from Elizabeth
Cady Stanton: "Thus came Lucretia Mott to me, at a period in my
young days when all life's problems seemed inextricably tan-
gled; . . . I often longed to meet some woman who had sufficient
confidence in herself to have and hold an opinion in the face of
opposition, a woman who understood the deep significance of life
to whom I could talk freely; my longings were answered at last."[1] I
think many woman historians of the seventeenth and eighteenth
centuries have felt that way about female Friends. We may feel this
affinity because Quaker women were deeply and actively engaged
in every phase of Quaker development from the inception of the
movement, and we admire them for their effort and commitment.
Perhaps we also are influenced by the historian's foresight, and we
know that we are watching the work of the prototypes of an
abolitionist and suffragist group of nineteenth-century women. Or
perhaps our interest is simply professional; they have left behind

such a gloriously rich record of themselves that we can know them individually and as a group, whereas most other women of the period are much more remote and their lives harder to recover.

American Quaker roots were in the English Civil War, in its exultant religious strivings and iconoclasm. Seventeenth-century English radical sects, which rejected ordained ministers in favor of those directly inspired by God, were particularly open to female participation, but few leaders were as specific as George Fox in their invitation to women to join in defining the movement. And few were as unbiased by gender as were the Quakers in their theological position in respect to female prophecy and the spiritual equality of women; as definitive as the Quakers in the creation of a special structure for regular female participation in public affairs; nor as exceptional in the portrayal of a couple (George Fox and Margaret Fell, a very atypical couple) as founders of the sect.

George Fox at the very beginning entrusted his Truth to a ministry by women; his first convert, Elizabeth Hooton, was no mere follower but an active preacher, and many of the "First Publishers of the Truth" were female. Margaret Fell, the founding mother, was a woman of much higher social status than Fox, and their marriage is an interesting symbol of the Quaker's sense of a spiritual equality that could demolish difference in class and even, perhaps, in gender. William Penn serves as another example of a Quaker leader who had a special affinity for deeply religious women, whom he identified as religious leaders, although he may have preferred and felt more comfortable with women who were his social peers; his affection and admiration of Margaret Fell were very great, too, and her opinion was important to him. And finally, according to Hugh Barbour, those early Quakers combined the roles of the "prophetess" and the "mother of Israel" in the female ministers who counselled and nurtured.[2] This was an interesting conception that may have smoothed the way to understanding a new female role in religion and prefigured some special effects of that religious role on Quaker family values and family formation, which have been observed by American historians of eighteenth-century Quakerism.

In 1653, Fox spelled out his position on spiritual equality—"For man and woman were helpsmeet, in the image of God and in

Righteousness and holiness, in the dominion before they fell; but after the Fall, in the transgression, the man was to rule over his wife. But in the restoration by Christ into the image of God and His righteousness and holiness again, in that they are helpsmeet, man and woman, as they were before the Fall."[3] This ebullient rejection of the curse of Genesis was enthusiastically endorsed by women, most notably by Margaret Fell in 1666 in "Womens Speaking Justified."[4] According to Fell's most recent biographer, Bonnelynn Young Kunze, who has studied Fell in the context of the history of women and specifically in respect to the history of female Friends, we should also credit Margaret Fell with the founding of the meetings for women.[5] It was certainly Sarah Fell, Margaret's daughter, who composed the remarkable epistle in the 1670s describing the fellowship of men and women ("for we are all the children of God by faith in Christ Jesus, where there is neither male nor female &c. but we are all one in Christ Jesus") and laying down the functions of women's meetings.[6]

Women's meetings were not easily instituted, however, and the Wilkinson-Story controversy developed out of resistance to the granting of authority to women over "clearness" to marry or discipline members. It took, apparently, the unusual energies of a Margaret Fell to keep the women's meetings going as Quakerism took on greater structural strength. By 1707, according to Kunze, a hardening of attitudes toward women's participation in English Quaker governance had emerged, women were discouraged from speaking, and their authority seems to have decayed, a pattern seen elsewhere when radical sects once open to women became more formal. Barry Levy also notes that when the Welsh Quakers first came to America, they appear to have had more conventional attitudes toward women.[7] But according to a Friend's record, 36 percent of traveling Friends who visited America between 1656 and 1701 were women, and from 1702 to 1760 the percentage was 33 percent, suggesting that women continued to be active at least in the ministry to America.

The first female Friends to come to America were women like Mary Dyer, who was willing to risk her life for the Truth. But she was not, in fact, very different from other English Friends of the time. The real American Quaker society was established at the end of the seventeenth century, when significant numbers came to settle in the colonies. And if there was decay in female authority in England by the end of the seventeenth century, it did not take place in the Quaker settlement in America, where the establishment of women's meetings was not particularly controversial and where the men generally respected the decisions of the women's meetings. In fact, the most vigorous period of creation of women's meetings in America would appear to have coincided with their decline in England. It is interesting that the American meeting structure was fairly quickly given architectural expression, too, when the meetings began in the early eighteenth century to build houses with an interesting system of sliding panels that could divide a large room for general meetings into two smaller ones for women's and men's meetings. English Friends did not generally create such special, segregated but equal spatial arrangements. They were, of course, legally constrained against building meeting houses during most of the seventeenth century, and in the eighteenth century women's meetings were less important to the men. However, English meetings were for the most part held in the seventeenth century in private homes where women, in ordinary domestic surroundings, undoubtedly felt particularly comfortable.

Another enormous difference between American and English Quakers was their respective positions in the larger social context. English Quakers were always a small minority who shared with other groups an unequal contest with the state religion; under those circumstances there was a powerful temptation to retreat even from active proselytizing to a more withdrawn and centered organization. In this situation, an uneasy toleration was the most anyone could hope for during the seventeenth and eighteenth centuries, although the place of English Quakers in the expanding commercial community was certainly of great significance in their self-definition and their individual economic growth.

Americans, however, had a different experience. In Pennsylvania and West Jersey they were in control of the government, which gave them special confidence about their own message at least until the middle of the eighteenth century. And just as the English Quakers were withdrawing into the structure of meetings, Americans were using the meeting structure to control their new environment, discipline a migrant population, and create a family base for a new society. Only after the Seven Years War would their social situation resemble the English one, and when that happened it would have been possible for women's meetings to lose some authority. We don't really know whether they did or not; however, it may be significant that as late as 1751 Abigail Pike and Rachel Wright founded a meeting on the North Carolina frontier. We do know that individual Quaker women were powerfully active in the great social movements of the early nineteenth century.

I think, then, that it is safe to conclude, to use a phrase popular among feminists today, that Quaker women were "empowered" from the beginning to take an active role in development of the belief system and the governance of the sect, that they were encouraged to engage publicly as Mothers of Israel, and that this makes them unusually interesting to us. It is also reasonably clear that the American experience of Quaker women, whose English roots are fully observable, was significantly different from the English experience in that female authority endured in the meeting structure, where women were involved in the family disciplines that were essential in a new society.

It is worth pointing out that the interest we take in Quaker women today is hardly new, although it is different. Quakers from the very beginning were terrific record keepers, and women were both keepers of records and their subjects. As women's meetings were instituted their members would buy record books, appoint a clerk (who had to be able to write) and get down to business. Their records are now an enormously important source for studying Quaker women.

The Quakers earliest, consciously historical writing is seen in their special concern for biography, a concern that did not discriminate against women. At first, they wanted to record life stories that concentrated on spiritual triumphs over oppression, persecution, and suffering. Joseph Besse's *A Collection of the Sufferings of the People Called Quakers,* the Quaker version of John Foxe's *Book of Martyrs,* is a splendid collection of short life stories of terrible hardship, and it includes many accounts of the experiences of women.[8] Of equal interest were the records of spiritual journeys, which were biographical if out of the ordinary mode. Finally, they began to create little biographies of truth's Friends, folks whose lives were worth preserving for themselves as well as for the lessons they could teach later generations. And many of these good people were women, of course. The *Friends' Miscellany*[9] and *A Quaker Post-bag*[10] are full of these: a modern version might be *Quaker Biographical Sketches*[11] edited by Willard Heiss. The intention behind these collections was to show how the sum of the whole can be reached by looking at the parts, and they are therefore similar—if less methodical—to contemporary prosopographical work.

This Quaker instinct for biography is also reflected in the appearance of some fuller-scale biographies of Quaker women written in the twentieth century. Two examples might be the study of Hannah Penn by Sophie Drinker[12] and the earlier but more ambitious and successful study of Margaret Fell by Isabel Ross.[13] These works were only marginally connected with what we would now call the history of women, but were important to it because of the need for biography as a first stage in the development of the history of women. We needed to fish some women out of the waters of time before we dared generalize about women's experience. Later biographies, for example the new study of Margaret Fell by Bonnelynn Kunze, or Margaret Bacon's work on Lucretia Mott,[14] are formed out of contemporary understandings of women's experience, and therefore offer more profound and sophisticated analyses of individual lives in a larger social context.

But modern biographical work came more neatly to match the earlier Quaker endeavors with the publication of *Notable American Women*.[15] This was an extraordinary event in the development of the history of women and in our understanding of Quaker women. I remember Edwin Bronner's showing me the list he had made of Quaker women who were included in *Notable American Women* as well as the force of our initial conclusions about their role in both abolition and the women's movement. Carol and John Stoneburner published that list in *The Influence of Quaker Women on American History*,[16] and further prosopographical work has been done by Margaret Bacon in *As the Way Opens: The Story of Quaker Women in America*.[17] The most detailed and rigorous research dealing quantitatively with Quaker women has been done by Jean Soderlund in "Women's Authority in Colonial Pennsylvania and New Jersey

Quaker Meetings, 1680–1760."[18] We can see a line, then, from the Quaker instinct for biography, to biography as an early and late phase of the history of women, to prosopography, which led to a deeper understanding of the achievements and leadership of Quaker women as a group, notable both for what they did and how they did it. All of this leads us to ask why these women were leaders, and why they were leaders in numbers that were out of proportion to their part of the female population as a whole.

What was there about Quakerism that led to this unusual female development? Here I think historians have been greatly affected by the development by cultural anthropologists of theories about public and private roles and their correlation with the degree to which gender is used to define roles. The conclusion that in societies in which gender is most important in defining roles men will dominate in the public sphere was most strikingly borne in on me by the work of Michelle Rosaldo and Louise Lamphere, but there are many other sources for it. It was this theory which shaped my own work on Quaker women in the 1970s[19], and informed comparisons I made between Puritans, among whom gender roles were more highly differentiated, and Quakers, who probably had the least differentiation of any group in the American colonies. I think it is implicit in Margaret Hope Bacon's *Mothers of Feminism*[20], one of the very few works that tries to deal with the whole history of American Quaker women. Bacon is concerned with change over time, and concentrates on gender equality, which she sees as empowering in a specifically political and public way, with Quaker women very much in the vanguard in the move by women into the public sphere. And so were Quaker historians. For example, Edwin Bronner in "An Early Example of Political Action by Women" identified women among the signers of a petition in 1696 to the Philadelphia Grand Jury. They wanted to stop boys and young men from public gambling, and Bronner pointed out in 1954 that those women had acted in a way that was out of the ordinary in the broader colonial context, but not in the Quaker context.[21]

Jean Soderlund, in "Women's Authority," provides an important corrective to this point of view. Although Soderlund is interested in the sources of the powerful activism of Quaker women in the late eighteenth and nineteenth centuries, she believes that if we

77

insist on "a conceptual framework that makes autonomous female power the standard" by which we judge Quaker women's experience, we do them a disservice—because they experienced great authority but not autonomy, which they wouldn't have wanted or understood. Nevertheless, her conclusions about the results of the period of the Seven Years War are similar to mine; that is, she also concludes that when men backed out of their public, political role in Pennsylvania and New Jersey, men and women were able to limit their concerns to the same things, and undertake action through the same agencies, on reasonably equal (but not autonomous) terms.

The areas in which gender equality in the colonial period have been sought by Margaret Bacon and more tentatively by me, and Quaker authority by Jean Soderlund, are commonly recognized. They are the Quaker belief system, which was liberating for women in many ways; the ministry, which was open to women; experience in ministry and meeting in public speaking; the experience of the conduct of public affairs in the women's meetings, including some economic initiative; education; and the emergence of women Friends into political action in ways that were acceptable to at least some Friends.

This has all been fruitful, but it has also produced a rather skewed view of its own. First, the focus on gender roles and activity in the public sphere, with its emphasis (even as corrected by Soderlund) on looking for the parallels between male and female roles, to some extent ignores the purely female experience of life; and, second, the invitation of the evidence to think of Quaker women as different from others, supported by the pleasure Quakers take in thinking of themselves as "peculiar people," tends to lead us to ignore the ways in which Quaker women might fit into the general American context. Looking for these common threads also leads us to ignore, or fail to appreciate, variations in Quaker experience. Finally, in all of these areas, including consideration of sources of gender equality, there is work to be done.

We might begin with the Quaker belief system as it applied to and was liberating for women. I think we are ready for a systematic analysis of the principal texts, both English and American, and for investigation into questions of how they were interpreted and applied. I would like to see something that would take me from Fox through Hicks, with special attention to Robert Barclay on Saint Paul; with an examination of divergences in attitudes towards women in England and America, in Orthodox and Hicksite communities, and in the several American regions where there were appreciable congregations of Quaker women. The materials for this study are considerable, and the subject is one of historical importance. The history of religion has few examples of liberated, Christian ways of thinking about women, their spirituality, and their role in the church, in connection with a successful and ultimately acceptable religious movement.

We have a lot of evidence, both anecdotal and spiritual, about women in the ministry, and this too could now be organized and analyzed more effectively to get a deeper look at their purposes, experiences, and effect. We have been more concerned with their bravery and spiritual drive than with the example they set, their language, the changes in their missions over time, their number, the places they visited, their spirituality, their rewards—we should look more deeply at Barry Levy's suggestion that, in the Delaware Valley at least, entry into the ministry brought status and marriage into a higher economic class. I suspect, too, that what some readers see as the largely uninformative journals of many of these ministers might give up more secrets to careful textual analysis. Carol Edkins in "Quest for Community: Spiritual Autobiographies of Eighteenth-Century Quaker and Puritan Women in America,"[22] and Joan M. Jensen in *Loosening the Bonds: Mid-Atlantic Farm Women, 1750–1850*[23] have made good beginnings here.[24]

Also, we are starting to develop an appreciable body of work on women's local and regional meetings. The most significant research to date is by Jean Soderlund, who has analyzed the leadership of selected meetings as well as the functions of those women's meetings. On a much smaller scale, Valerie Gladfelter has done some work on discipline[25] and Susan Forbes on committee assignments and marriages.[26] Jack Marietta's work on discipline between 1748 and 1783 is a particularly rich and rewarding thematic approach to a large group of meetings, which is not confined to but includes the work of women's meetings and uses gender as a variable in analysis of discipline. Marietta also examines the relationship between discipline and the reform movement of the mid-eighteenth century, which both pulled the Quaker community inward and detached them from the political process. Here he is somewhat less concerned with the special implications for women, but Soderlund takes full account of his work.[27]

But the very inclination to see the Quakers as a different or "peculiar" people, or as Marietta puts it, Quakerism as a "sanctuary for odd, holy men and women" is in some ways a deterrent to seeing Friends in the larger American context in which they lived. In comparing Quakers and Puritans I have tried in a small way to demonstrate the utility of working a larger canvas, as have Richard Dunn and I in the volume of essays on *The World of William Penn*.[28] Nancy Tomes's splendid article on visiting patterns of Quaker women uses a Quaker case to help explain the evolution of the modern American family.[29]

Two historians have been principally concerned with the history of the Quaker family and its place in American development. J. William Frost published his path-breaking work, *The Quaker Family in Colonial America* in 1973.[30] In it, he took the view that the spiritual equality enjoyed by women did not extend beyond the meeting; but he did pay a great deal of attention to women and their role in marriage and childbearing, devoted to maintaining the sect by proper education and socialization of children. He located by the end of the eighteenth century a special and modern relationship between Quaker mother and child. His book, incidentally, was one of the earliest to include the word "women" in the index. More recently, Barry Levy has been reassessing the history of family in the Delaware Valley. His approach is truly comparative; he sets the Quaker family in the context of the literature on the development of the modern family; and he devotes a great deal of attention to Quaker women whose communal authority, he believes, rested in their role as mothers in a family system based on nurturance, affection, and support during the eighteenth century. He concludes that many Quaker women in the Delaware Valley "harmonized the roles of wife, minister, and mother into a novel and influential feminine mystique" in which they were needed for marriage and family discipline, while at the same time, a child-centered economy applied unusual economic restraints on women in order to preserve property for the children.[31]

There is one further point about Quaker history that should be made: The female role and biographical instinct that were part of the earliest experiences of Quakers have resulted in a set of historical records in which women are present in a way that is simply not the case for the rest of colonial America. Furthermore, women appear under their own names (the "John Smith's wife" kind of naming is notably absent) and they kept many of their own records so that they are not constantly being seen through male eyes. This in turn, has led to the writing of history that is integrated in its own way. That is, women as actors are frequently and appreciatively cited, even when women's concerns are not treated in a specific way. Arthur Worrall's *Quakers in the Colonial Northeast* describes the work of many brave women; for example, those early messengers of truth who both endured persecution and provided it, like Mary Dyer; or, to take another sort of case, Anne Bell, who promoted a separation in Rhode Island over meeting authority; or again, Mary Weston who came from England between 1750 and 1752 and preached to thousands in something of the style of George Whitefield. However, the words "women" or "women's meeting" do not appear in Worrall's index.[32]

The final area I want to treat is related to a point made earlier; that is, in seeking to understand gender equality we have looked to parallel structures and perhaps neglected to pay adequate attention to the truly female experience of life among Friends. Carroll Smith-Rosenberg has for some time been telling us how we can uncover and appreciate women's experience in a "female world of love and ritual"[33]; and it may be that if biography was our first phase of women's history and the search to understand the conditions of gender equality was our second phase, then our coming of age will be the attempt to understand women's experience for itself and in the context of its time.

Hugh Barbour, Jean Soderlund, Jerry Frost, and Barry Levy have all, in their separate ways, looked at women's experience in the context of the Society of Friends, both in ministry and governance, and in the family order, unusual in its time, which emerged at least in part from the inclusion of women in spiritual order. One place in which we can see a bridge from spiritual order to domesticity is in meeting-house architecture. There has recently been considerable attention paid to domestic architecture in the sixteenth and seventeenth centuries. Historians have looked at the new divisions of household space, with rooms set aside for specific functions that were assigned to women. More and more, then, household space was being defined as female space. This development was well under way by the time American Quakers began to build their houses for meetings, which they made to look very much like family houses. There was a definite transfer of ideas from the domestic scene to the meeting house, which is especially evident in the spatial arrangement for the women's meeting for business that combined a woman's space with a woman's sphere. Furthermore, the seventeenth century saw the beginning of the drawing of a boundary between the house (women's space and shared space) and either field or counting house (men's space, not usually shared). When Quakers built their meeting houses as reflections of domestic architecture, they reinforced women's authority by putting up buildings that were recognizably domestic and therefore evidently belonging to women and to family.

We know that American women of all classes in the eighteenth century spent enormous amounts of time sewing, and consequently they were greatly invested in what they wore. Amelia Mott Gummere in 1901 wrote *The Quaker: A Study in Costume,* the only extended examination we have of Quaker dress.[34] Like many Americans since, Friends proclaimed their membership and their peculiarity through dress, and dress was also a crucial statement of moral positions. Gummere had excellent sources to draw on, including numerous recommendations from one meeting to another or from a woman in the ministry. Hannah Hill in 1726 cautioned against hoops, red heels, and bare breasts among other things, and insisted on the Quaker apron, "That we might be unto the Lord, A Chosen Generation, A Royal Priesthood, An Holy Nation, A Peculiar People," a heady recipe.[35] It would be extremely interesting to revisit the subject of dress using the insights of the anthropologists.

We are more fortunate in knowing a good deal about how rural Friends spent their time, and to what effect, because of Joan M.

Jensen's *Loosening the Bonds: Mid-Atlantic Farm Women, 1750–1850.*
Much of her evidence comes from the nineteenth century, with the
result that she provides us with the first investigation into the links
between the earlier movement, the period of reformation, and the
nineteenth century. Her book is an illuminating venture into wom-
en's work and their trade. She does not ignore their public work in
the ministry, and even links with the older tradition by including a
brief biography of a farm woman who also developed a mine on
her property and had time, too, to help runaway slaves. We now
need a similar examination, for the same time period, of urban
women Friends.

Nancy Tomes's study of visiting patterns is also an effort to
examine women's experience and its significance, and it was written in direct response to Smith-Rosenberg's challenge. Tomes's
conclusions about the centrality of religious affiliation and kinship
in the creation of female networks helps to explain both Quaker
female experience of life and the evolution of the modern family.
It, too, is a good example of what can be done given the richness of
the Quaker records.

At the same time, there are some deep and unresolved mysteries.
Let us consider just one. Robert Wells's demographic work has
shown us that in the eighteenth century Quaker women married
somewhat later and were limiting the number of children they
had.[36] This certainly can be explained by the emphasis placed on
intimate and affectionate family life and a desire to preserve property for children. Joan Jensen discusses these issues in connection
with rural families. But how do we explain an increase in celibacy?
Did it result from an increase in the number of female Friends over
male Friends, combined with strictures against marrying out? Is
Barry Levy right in believing that it was poor children who could
not find mates? Or was there something else going on in the
Quaker world of women? Certainly, Friends were tolerant of unmarried women, which was unusual in the eighteenth century, but
who, having read Sarah Wister's diary, is not astonished to dis-
cover that the young flirt never married.[37]

We have learned a great deal about Quaker women, and they
have given us inestimable help. But amongst other things we do
not know, it is not clear why they were driven to record their

present for the future. What special sense of history did they have? Did it manifest itself in other ways amongst Friends? Distinctively amongst women? Until this deeper philosophical meaning can be uncovered, we will have to satisfy ourselves with the conclusion that it is reassuring to learn how much there is still to do to understand fully just one small population of American colonial women. Because after all, historian's work, like women's work, is never done.

NOTES

1. Elizabeth Cady Stanton et al., *History of Woman Suffrage* (New York: Fowler and Wells, 1881), 1:419.

2. Hugh Barbour, "Quaker Prophetesses and Mothers in Israel," in J. William Frost and John M. Moore, eds., *Seeking the Light* (Wallingford, Pa.: Pendle Hill Publications, and Haverford, Pa.: Friends Historical Association, 1986), 41–60.

3. George Fox, *A Collection of Many Select and Christian Epistles,* Printed and sold by T. Sowle, 1698), 2:323.

4. Margaret Askew Fell, *Womens speaking justified* . . . (London: 1666).

5. Bonnelyn Young Kunze, "The Family, Social and Religious Life of Margaret Fell," Ph.D. diss., University of Rochester, 1986.

6. Milton D. Speizman and Jane C. Kronick, eds., "A Seventeenth-Century Quaker Women's Declaration," *SIGNS,* 1 (1975): 235.

7. Barry Levy, *Quakers and the American Family: British Settlement in the Delaware Valley* (New York: Oxford University Press, 1988).

8. Joseph Besse, *A Collection of the Sufferings of the People Called Quakers* (London: L. Hinde, 1753).

9. John and Isaac Comly, eds., *Friends' Miscellany,* vols. 1–12, 1831–1839. (Philadelphia: William Sharpless, 1831–1839).

10. Sophie Felicité Locker-Lampson, ed., *A Quaker Post-bag* (London: Longmans Green, 1910).

11. Willard Heiss, ed., *Quaker Biographical Sketches of Ministers and Elders* (Indianapolis, Ind.: published for the author, 1972).

12. Sophie Lewis Hutchinson Drinker, *Pennsylvania's Honoured Mistress.* Paper read before the Welcome Society, 1959.

13. Isabel Ross, *Margaret Fell: Mother of Quakerism* (York, England: William Sessions, Ebor Press, 1984; reprint of 1949 edition).

14. Margaret Hope Bacon, *Valiant Friend* (New York: Walker, 1980).

15. Edward T. James and Janet Wilson James, eds., *Notable American Women 1607–1950* (Cambridge: Belknap Press of Harvard University Press, 1971).

16. Carol and John Stoneburner, eds., *The Influence of Quaker Women on American History* (Lewiston, N.Y.: E. Mellen, 1986).

17. Margaret Hope Bacon, *As the Way Opens* (Richmond, Ind.: Friends United Press, 1980).

18. Jean Soderlund, "Women's Authority in Pennsylvania and New Jersey Quaker Meetings, 1680–1760," *William and Mary Quarterly,* 3d series, 44 (1987): 722–749.

19. Mary Maples Dunn, "Women of Light," in Carol Ruth Berkin and Mary Beth

Document

Norton, eds., *Women of America: A History* (Boston: Houghton Mifflin, 1979), 114–136, and "Saints and Sisters: Congregational and Quaker Women in the Early Colonial Period," in Janet Wilson James, ed., *Women in American Religion* (Philadelphia: University of Pennsylvania Press, 1980), 27–46.

20. Margaret Hope Bacon, *Mothers of Feminism* (San Francisco: Harper & Row, 1986).

21. Edwin B. Bronner, "An Early Example of Political Action by Women," *Bulletin of the Friends Historical Association,* 43 (1954): 29–32.

22. Carol Edkins, "Quest for Community: Spiritual Autobiographies of Eighteenth-Century Quaker and Puritan Women in America," in Estelle Jelinek, ed., *Women's Autobiography: Essays in Criticism* (Bloomington: University of Indiana Press, 1980).

23. Joan M. Jensen, *Loosening the Bonds* (New Haven: Yale University Press, 1986).

24. Rebecca D. Larson, Harvard University, is writing a doctoral dissertation on women ministers, with a special focus on trans-Atlantic ministries.

25. Valerie G. Gladfelter, "Power Challenged," in Michael Zuckerman, ed., *Friends and Neighbors* (Philadelphia: Temple University Press, 1982).

26. Susan S. Forbes, "Quaker Tribalism," in Zuckerman, *Friends and Neighbors.*

27. Jack D. Marietta, *The Reformation of American Quakerism* (Philadelphia: University of Pennsylvania Press, 1984).

28. Richard S. Dunn and Mary Maples Dunn, eds., *The World of William Penn* (Philadelphia: University of Pennsylvania Press, 1986).

29. Nancy Tomes "The Quaker Connection," in Zuckerman, *Friends and Neighbors.*

30. J. William Frost, *The Quaker Family in Colonial America* (New York: St. Martin's Press, 1973).

31. Barry Levy, *Quakers and the American Family.*

32. Arthur Worrall, *Quakers in the Colonial Northeast* (Hanover, N.H.: University Press of New England, 1980).

33. Carroll Smith-Rosenberg, *Disorderly Conduct* (New York: Knopf, 1985).

34. Amelia Mott Gummere, *The Quaker: a Study in Costume* (New York: B. Blom, 1968).

35. Berkin and Norton, *Women of America,* 135.

36. Robert V. Wells, "Quaker Marriage Patterns in a Colonial Perspective," in Nancy F. Cott and Elizabeth H. Pleck, eds., *A Heritage of Her Own* (New York: Simon and Schuster, 1979).

37. Sarah Wister, *The Journal and Occasional Writings of Sarah Wister,* ed. Kathryn Zabelle Derounian (Rutherford: Fairleigh Dickinson University Press, 1987).

DOCUMENT

Ann Cooper Whitall (1716–1797) wrote a journal that was never meant for our eyes. Fortunately she heeded the Quaker dictum to keep a record of her spiritual life, and a rudimentary literacy permitted her to do so, because her journal speaks in poignant terms of the hardship of frontier life in the eighteenth century. Ann Whitall lived about a day's journey from Philadelphia in Haddonfield, New Jersey, but she faced isolation, was frightened by Indians and disease, and needed spiritual consolation to combat loneliness and depression. A traveling minister, Mary Kirby, supplied spiritual uplift. This journal reveals what women's ministry to women meant.

Michael C. Osborne produced the original transcription of the journal in 1977 while an undergraduate student at Haverford College. This transcription is available in the Quaker Collection at Haverford College. Spelling and punctuation have been modernized here.

Journal, 1760

10th day of the Third Month. Mary Kirby[1] was at Meeting, a small Meeting if ever I saw but a good Meeting; I hope, to all at Haddonfield [New Jersey] today.

6th day, to Meeting. A good Meeting also. Oh, that we might always be worthy of a good Meeting.

First day, at home and right cold; and such a snow hasn't been since the hard winter nineteen years ago—two feet high and six inches, some say. What a snow for the poor dumb creatures. Oh, I often think if the people suffered instead of the poor cattle!

16th day of the Third Month—[the snow] is one foot thick now.

20th day, Oh, the dismal news of the Indians' killing of the white people! I must write down some of the dreams I had dreamed when I was a girl above 20 years ago, about the Indians' killing of me more than once. Now if it ain't me yet, I don't know how soon it may be my turn, and my poor children. Oh, I often think, how can people be so full of laughing and prating and lay nothing to heart? It seems enough to make us to grieve and mourn. Always we go to bed [with] what grieves us, [then] we get up and go about our business. How many times a day do we praise His mighty name that gives peace and plenty to us? Do we praise His mighty name three times a day, as often as we eat? Or sit down and not think of Him that gave it? Oh, what a poor crew we are! I say, praises be to him that gives us everything we eat and drink. Oh, praises, praises be to His mighty name all the day long.

6th day. It is Quarterly Meeting at Haddonfield, and Mary [Kirby] is there. It grieves me much because I can't go, but Job is so bad I don't know but he will die.[2]

7th day. Mother, brother James and David and sister Sarah

Brown are all here from Henry Wood's burial.[3] John Storer was at Haddonfield with Mary Kirby and they spoke much of the afflication [that] is come and coming upon us, of death parting of so many husbands from wives, and wives from husbands, and children from parents.[4] Our Job is so bad yet we don't know how it will go with him.

6th day. It is the ninth day he has been sick. It is a trying time to us when we think we must part and never see a child no more. Oh, that we may all remember this time among us now. We have seven children but so many people dying, both old and young, we can't expect to live long together. Joshua Wood died with the same ailment Job has, and Henry Wood last 7th day was buried. He lay eight days [ill].

Now it is the 28th of the Third Month and [John] Lord with us all night.[5] Hannah Ladd[6] with us the night before.

2nd day. Job is in a poor dead condition. He lies still. Now he is better, 4th day.

2nd day of the 4th Month, 1760.

A Fifth Day, it is two weeks since he was took sick.

6th day. I went to John Ladd's to hear how he does with the small pox away at Amboy.

First Day to Meeting—a poor dead condition some of the time. Oh, this enemy of our souls and this ain't all the trouble I have, for if the children and I am at home, their father won't stay at home (not three First Days in the whole year if he can help it). I often thinks if I run gadding about so as he does what sort of a house should we keep? Oh what sort of a pattern is this, oh, [when] waiting upon the Lord and setting to meditate in his presence? I think it is more to be desired than any company in the world.

10th day of the 4th Month, our dear friend Mary Kirby was here at Woodbury and Elizabeth Smith from Burlington, New Jersey, and she spoke first, and spoke as if some was likely for [to] miss their way by not giving heed to the Inward Guide.[7] Oh, what a sad case is this; then Mary told us of sleeping in Meeting. She felt it among us, some would dress like others and go like them to Meeting but that would not do for they would be like the Foolish Virgins [who] had no oil in their lamps. She told us of them over and over again with a great deal of sorrow. What did we do for ourselves she said, when we were asleep? Oh, this part that never dies. I rejoiced to hear her tell us of sleeping in Meeting! Being in great hopes it might do some good. Desiring I might be favored with a sense of my own condition and see my own failings. And she told us of the warnings we have had many times from sometimes [ago when] we were in a little. Oh, or dread when one did die out of the house. We could think then that we must go hence. But that would be all forgot. We live in plenty, she said, we did not want bread. Oh, what a hard thing would that be, we did not know, no, how soon that would be. Oh, that we might be thankful receivers of all these wonderful favors and blessings we have of the Mighty One. She said there was many a cold home and she did believe there would be more cold homes. Oh, prepare, prepare for this change. We know it must come and we know not how soon and how can we be so dead?

She got up again and spoke so to the afflicted ones [that they] be so afflicted every way that [they] knew not what to do nor which way to turn but it was often her lot to be so overwhelmed in sorrow and in grief. Well, she said, the world loved its own but not the sorrowful and mourners; well, in this sorrowful condition she said was the time to say Glory, Glory to His Mighty Name that brings sorrow. Oh come death, come life, come what will, come, we will serve the Above. All, oh glory, glory to His Mighty Name. She said, oh, these mourners that have no comfort in nothing that they think is not a serving of their Mighty Maker.

First day. I think there is no comfort anywhere. Nothing but sorrow at home and abroad.

3rd day. I did not know but we should have the house blown down over our heads for such a storm I never saw. Oh, is it not enough to make every one to tremble when we don't know but every minute will be the last. But as soon as it is over then to laugh and mischief again. Oh, oh, what will make the world to leave wickedness? Oh, my heart has ached this day and I am full of sorrow and indeed I always am in fishing time, for I think there is so much drinking and play and prating that there can't be so much good in their heads.[8] I haven't sold them any cider yet. I have most[ly] peas to sell them.

Document

[1]Mary Ransome Kirby (1709–1779) was born in Norfolk, England. Widowed in 1739, she travelled to preach to Friends both sides of the Atlantic Ocean for the next thirty years. See *Dictionary of Quaker Biography* (in typescript), Quaker Collection, Haverford College, for this biographical note and those that follow.

[2]Smallpox was rampant.

[3]These are Ann's relatives. James lived from 1720 to 1789 and David lived from 1724 to 1795; David also kept a spiritual diary. Sarah Cooper Brown lived from 1722 to 1774. Sarah Whitall was the aunt of Ann Cooper Whitall's husband, James. She married Henry Wood in 1715.

[4]John Storer (1715–1795) was accepted as a member of the Society of Friends in 1748 in England. In 1760 he began a ministry in the American colonies.

[5]Joshua Lord (1698–1760) was recognized as a Quaker minister in 1727. He was born near Woodbury, New Jersey.

[6]Hannah and John Ladd were neighbors of Ann Cooper Whitall.

[7]Elizabeth Smith (1724–1772) was born in Burlington, New Jersey. She began preaching at the age of twenty-one years.

[8]Probably the shad running in the Delaware River.

THREE

The Nineteenth Century

NANCY A. HEWITT

The Fragmentation of Friends: The Consequences for Quaker Women in Antebellum America

IN 1921, Rufus M. Jones declared that the "greatest tragedy of Quaker history was the separation of the Society in America, in 1827–28," which broke "the once united and harmonious body of Friends into two unsympathetic and misunderstanding branches, both shorn of power."[1] In the most recent study of the schism, published in 1986, H. Larry Ingle concluded similarly. He labelled his story of the divisions among five groups of Quakers "a sad one," claiming that "anytime well-intentioned believers fall out over relatively trivial differences in belief and tear apart long-standing friendships and even family relations, tragedy can only result."[2]

This "tragedy" of the 1827–1828 schism was followed by less dramatic but apparently no less damaging divisions between Gurneyites and Wilburites and between Hicksites and Progressives in the 1840s. Quaker historians seem uniformly to agree that the thirty years from 1825 to 1855 were "the darkest and saddest in the history of Quakerism."[3]

Yet schism, division, and upheaval, particularly in the religious arena, have not been uniformly deplored by historians of women. As Sherin Marshall Wyntjes writes of the Protestant Reformation, women "found themselves participating in political and economic turmoil. Their emotional and practical support was essential to the Protestant cause. Consequently," Wyntjes argues, "they took on new roles in an unsettled situation." Only "as the movement triumphed and became institutionalized" were women excluded from active participation.[4] Lyle Koehler's study of women's roles in the antinomian turmoil of the colonial era similarly highlights the opportunity for female leadership to emerge when "the spiritual and secular status quo" are challenged.[5] Finally, in his study of the English Civil War sects, Keith Thomas demonstrates that "in the sects [including Quakers], women played a disproportionate role; they received from them correspondingly greater opportunities."[6]

These three authors all point to similar theological themes as the basis for women's more active role among the sectarians they studied. A "personal, non-hierarchic, lay dominated religion," an emphasis on both direct inspiration and scriptural authority, and a depreciation of the ministerial role promised women greater earthly as well as spiritual equality.[7] Yet these beliefs and practices only turned promises into reality during periods of upheaval and agitation. And each upheaval, as Wyntjes notes of the Reformation, "was followed by a time of retrenchment, when the progressive elements from the standpoint of women's possibilities were expunged from these movements."[8] This does not mean that women lost all the gains they had made, but rather that the creative expansion of the female sphere was curtailed as male authority within dissenting sects was reasserted.[9]

In the light of such testimony, this essay will reexamine the "tragedies" of the 1820s and 1840s to see if the consequences of schism might not have been more positive for Quaker women than for men. Such an interpretation would converge with those studies, beginning with Joan Kelly's analysis of the Renaissance, in which scholars have determined that the trajectory of men's and women's histories have often been at odds. In general, this has operated to deprive women of meaningful and positive change—in the Enlightenment, the American and French revolutions, and other periods of intellectual, social, and political progress. The Quaker schisms may provide a counter example—a historical moment when the disruption and decline of male authority was accompanied by the nurturance and expansion of women's power.

This essay is speculative rather than definitive. It seeks to raise issues rather than resolve them, in the hopes of inspiring further study of the fragmentation of Friends and the consequences for Quaker women. In addition, it seeks to expand upon the conventional interpretations of Quaker historians by emphasizing the external importance of internal disruption: for too long the debates among Quakers have been viewed as matters of concern only to the Society of Friends rather than to society at large. Most importantly for women's history, the disruptions of the early nineteenth century, which encouraged Quaker women to consider their place in the Society, led a significant minority to advocate woman's rights beyond its boundaries. These served as the vanguard of that much larger body of female Friends who became ardent feminists and pacifists in the twentieth century.

The sources for this investigation are voluminous. Here, I will rely first on the standard secondary accounts of the great separations, reading the events they describe from a gender-specific perspective. Then I will turn to a less familiar set of primary sources, the correspondence of the Amy and Isaac Post family of Long Island and Rochester, New York, in which the personal and familial repercussions as well as the social and political potential of Quaker schisms are revealed.

Jones sets the framework for many later studies, dividing early Quaker history into two periods. In the years 1648–1725, the movement to establish the Society of Friends is positive, apostolic, and catholic, focusing on the dissemination of information and the conversion of true believers. From 1725 to 1825, however, the Society became more timid and exclusive, its leaders cultivating already broken ground, thereby creating "a peculiar people" set off from the world.[10] From the beginning, women took full part in the public ministry, but they "did not have complete equality with the men" in the business affairs of the Society, which became increasingly important during the later era of retrenchment. In the ministry, moreover, at least by 1783, women and men could not travel "as companions in service, to avoid all occasions of offence thereby."[11]

Yet among itinerant ministers, particularly among those travelling to frontier areas, this did not diminish women's commitment to carry the Friends' message. Of those who "went out to rebuild the waste places," Sarah (Lyne) Grubb was "one of the most powerful women preachers of her time." During her visit to Ireland, she wrote, "The meetings here have been times of very deep digging; the spring of life lies low, and that of the ministry in unison with it; but through a great deal of labour, the power made its own way, even into some dominion, in each meeting."[12] Throughout the late eighteenth century, women like Sarah Grubb, Mary

Dudley, Catharine Phillips, Martha Routh, Sarah Elgar, Patience Brayton, Huldah Hoag, Rebecca Jones, Elizabeth Coggeshall, Sarah Harrison, and Hannah Barnard sustained the tradition of female preaching.

Despite the general quiescence in Quaker ranks in this period, it was the isolated pockets of upheaval that often formed the centers of women's influence. For instance, as southern Quakers in the United States wrestled with the institution of slavery, Sarah Harrison, accompanied by Norris Jones and Lydia Hoskins, travelled to the region, pleading for emancipation as the only conscientious course. And it was from this same region that two of North America's most controversial Quaker converts would come, Sarah and Angelina Grimke.

Another area of early nineteenth-century upheaval was Ireland. Sarah Grubb's visit there coincided with a defection that was "destined to be the precursor of still more serious events." The crisis suggested by the Irish controversy "came to light, as a result of the European visit of an American Quaker minister named Hannah Barnard." Barnard, who was disowned in 1802, was "the leading champion in the first years of the nineteenth century of a freer type of thought in the Society."[13] She was accompanied in her travels by Rhode Island Quaker Elizabeth Coggeshall.

Women friends were not arrayed only on the progressive side of the growing chasm, however. Rebecca Jones and Mary Dudley were two of the first wave of those Ingle calls "evangelical Quakers." American Quakers who had ministered in Europe, Jones and Dudley would return to their homeland where their preachings would fan if not ignite the flames of discord. In what would remain perhaps one of the few areas of agreement with their female theological foes, these evangelical women Friends admonished their sister parishoners to remember that the Society was "composed of females as well as males, who as like have a need to move under a sense of their own weakness."[14] These words could have as easily come from the mouths of Barnard or Coggeshall.

In the decade from 1818 to 1828, as the Society of Friends approached and then crossed the great divide, the men's meetings and male leaders directed the contending forces. Still, the Quaker desire for consensus and the need of each side for spiritual and practical support opened the way for women advocates. Priscilla Coffin Hunt and Mary Lukens were among the prominent Hicksite ministers, while Anna Braithwaite, Ann Jones, and Elizabeth Robson promoted the Orthodox cause. Moreover, within weekly, monthly, and quarterly meetings, individuals emerged who wielded the power of the women's meetings for the benefit of one faction or the other.

In the early 1820s, the Philadelphia meetings were already arenas of contention. At the end of December 1822, Elias Hicks, spiritual leader of the movement that was to bear his name, departed from the city, and the elders could not contain a collective sigh of relief. They were almost immediately confronted, however, with a new challenge, "a woman minister from Indiana whose theology parallelled Hicks's and whose appeal rivalled his." Wherever Priscilla Hunt appeared, "the meetinghouses overflowed with people unable to find seats."[15] Though her style did not attract plaudits from Philadelphia's ministers and elders, popular appeal sustained her ministry for four months.

Not all local women supported this Hicksite ministry. A woman elder at Philadelphia's Pine Street Meeting once refused to rise in prayer when Hunt signalled the proper moment by kneeling. Hunt's coworker John Mott was rebuked by a woman Friend and accused of "unprofitably draw[ing together] the lighter parts of Society at his meetings!"[16] A few months after Hunt's and Mott's excursions into Philadelphia, Anna Braithwaite arrived to promote the Orthodox cause. She "leaped into the fray and rapidly became one of the sharpest disputants." During this visit, Braithwaite visited Elias Hicks and then penned her thoughts on their conversation. Their discussion "focused the issues for a wide audience." And "thanks to the rapid circulation of copies of [Braithwaite's] memorandum . . . a barrage of pamphlets became available for anyone who wanted to participate vicariously in the discussion."[17]

From Jericho, Long Island, Mary Kirby Willis detailed the goings-on for her sisters Hannah and Amy in central New York, discussing Hicks's response to Braithwaite and the local monthly meeting's refusal to sustain a female member's ministry alongside the Orthodox English lady.[18] A constant stream of letters poured forth from Long Island and central New York women, describing and analyzing the latest events in the confrontations between Braith-waite and Hicks, almost all sympathetic to the famous reformer. Such sympathy did not arise, however, from any vaunted views of male authority, since these same correspondents also applauded the labors of Lucretia Mott and Priscilla Hunt.

At Green Street Meeting in Philadelphia, where the schism would first appear as a visible wound in the Society's body, women again gathered on both sides of the chasm.[19] Among the Hicksites, Abraham Lower provided the most persistent leadership. His wife Susan was also active, though we do not know to what extent her agitation parallelled his perseverance. More significantly, two women elders stood firm against the Hicksite wave as it broke over Green Street Meeting. Mary Taylor and Ann Scattergood along with Leonard Snowden were relieved of their duties as elders by the Monthly Meeting but supported for reinstatement by the Quarterly Meeting.

When the dispute remained unsettled, it was the women's meeting of Philadelphia Quarterly who sought a visitation committee to advise on the matter. And it was this committee that advised that Green Street Meeting be "set down" and its members transferred to nearby Northern Division. This decision, initiated by the women's action in 1826, led to schism in 1827.

In April of that year, anti-Hicksite Elizabeth Robson and Stephen Grellet descended on Green Street Meeting, and with their support, Taylor and Scattergood returned to reclaim their positions as elders. In the ensuing chaos, the men's meeting declared for secession from Philadelphia Quarterly meeting, but their sisters requested more time to consider the matter. Clerked by Scattergood, the women's meeting was proclaimed "seditious" by the Hicksite men. One reform-minded husband even entered the women's room and led his wife out by the hand.[20]

The presence of Robson, Scattergood, and Taylor postponed an immediate decision for secession among the women despite the hooting and jeering of the men. William Poole, frustrated by the delay, complained that the "women—'bad captive silly women laden with sin'—were giving the Society much trouble." He was convinced that some men could be found "*not standing firmly and uprightly* in consequence of the *influence of women*."[21] In this opinion, Poole captured the derisive attitude of many male Quakers toward their female opponents but also, ironically, granted such women significant power.

In New Jersey's Mt. Holly Monthly Meeting, it was the Orthodox majority's turn to deride the efforts of female opponents. When George Jones and Ann Jones descended upon Mt. Holly Meeting, they were confronted by Maria Imlay, who was "widely acclaimed by the reform set" but who had been disowned by the Orthodox.[22] Imlay had been removed as a minister in 1826 "after she preached that the 'light within' was the only means of redemption necessary." (Another female firebrand, Phebe Johnson, suffered a similar fate in New York for advocating the same position.)

While the men of Mt. Holly attempted to reconcile certain of their differences, Ann Jones and Maria Imlay squared off, the former declaring that she had "no fellowship" with the latter, and leaving the house without closing the meeting. Meanwhile, Hannah Post wrote to her sister Amy Kirby lamenting Anna Braithwaite's forthcoming visit to New York Yearly Meeting and claiming that it "will spoil the pleasure of being there by rousing diversity of sentiment."[23] Hannah, who died in 1827, would not live to see the Society fall prey to such diversity, but Amy and the rest of the family would remain embroiled in the bitter fallout for the next quarter century.

It would indeed spoil the pleasure of many a meeting, but the years of contention would also open the way for Amy and like-minded women to play a more central role in the shaping of their society. For as the schism spread, so did women's influence. In western meetings in particular, itinerant and resident women seem to have played a significant role. In 1828, Mary Lukens of Chester County, Pennsylvania, already a confirmed Hicksite, accompanied Elias Hicks to Ohio Meeting where a crucial debate on separation took place. She was a critical figure in the decision of the local women's meeting to secede. Similarly important were the labors of Priscilla Hunt, who after her first husband's death, "moved to frontier Indiana and developed a preaching style that mesmerized her rural audiences."[24] Though her personal tragedies were lamented by her sisters back east, her power as a preacher was thought to derive in part from these increased demands on her faith.

Within the new dissident meetings at which preachers like Hunt appeared, women attempted to institutionalize their reasserted equality. At the first Quarterly Meeting of Hicksites, where women formed roughly 40 percent of the participants, both sexes agreed to replace the old Meeting for Sufferings with a "representative committee" that would for the first time include women members. In addition, by limiting the powers of the ministers and elders, a bastion of male power in most Orthodox meetings, women gained greater equity with their Hicksite brethren. Yet Hicksites resisted more radical changes, wishing not to be "faulted for departing from Friends' principles" while trying to establish their new meetings as the true child of the original Society.[25]

In at least one instance, evidence suggests that women were less concerned with "the great importance, especially at the present time, of keeping strictly to the dicipline [sic]." When Amy Kirby and Isaac Post married "out of the order of Society," Amy being the younger sister of Isaac's deceased wife Hannah, their Long Island Monthly Meeting investigated both the couple and those attending the wedding. A sympathetic Friend reported that some members of the committee found Amy's responses in particular "a little too tart."[26] The following year, Amy's sister-in-law reported favorably on the ministry of a woman named Rhoda, noting especially her claim that "many are joined in wedloc [sic] that are not married in the true sense of the thing."[27] Some two decades later, at least one woman who started down the Hicksite path in the 1820s would conclude that a woman "ought to be better qualified to direct the spiritual life of her own sex than any belov'd disciple or even Jesus himself as a man or a brother."[28]

Throughout the 1830s and 1840s, Hicksite women asserted themselves at gatherings of the Society, applauded the preachings of Lucretia Mott, Priscilla Hunt Cadwallader, and other women, and extended their rights and powers within those local meetings where progress seemed possible.[29] Married women encouraged their single or widowed sisters to accompany more well-known female ministers for "a profitable season," and many complied.[30] Women also participated fully in the attempts from 1837 on in Rochester Monthly Meeting, Michigan Quarterly Meeting, and Genesee Yearly Meeting to liberalize the discipline. The proposed alterations would have further diminished the powers of elders and ministers, equalized the responsibilities of the men's and women's meetings, and allowed for greater participation in "worldly" reform associations. And, as in the 1820s, women also fully participated in the opposition to such measures.

Having detailed the schism of 1848 elsewhere and women's prominent roles in both the division and the new-found dissident faction of Congregational of Progressive Friends, I will not repeat the tale here.[31] It is worth noting, however, that women seceded from Genesee Yearly Meeting in numbers roughly equal to those of men and that they often preceeded their male kin in removing themselves from the Society. At least in some cases, withdrawals and disownments flowed through female kinship networks, as it did in the Post household. Mary Post Hallowell, Amy Post's stepdaughter, withdrew from fellowship in 1845 while her husband William remained a member of the Society until 1846, when his support of Mary's actions caused his disownment. Mary was joined in her departure by Amy, Amy 's husband Isaac, and Amy's younger sister Sarah Kirby Hallowell.

Perhaps women raised the suspicions of their elders sooner than did men, since their worldly actions were probably considered by the Society as more disruptive of the accepted order. Thus did (non-Quaker) abolitionist Lucy Colman relate that when "Mrs. Post, in company with the 'world's people,' left her home for the purpose of holding bazars [*sic*] or fairs to raise funds to carry on the Antislavery work," she came under the scrutiny of a committee of Friends. One of the objects of the committee's visitation "was to advise her in regard to her duty towards her family," which led Amy "to exhibit the contents of her stocking-bag—the store on hand being sixty-four pairs."[32]

It did not lead her to restrict her worldly labors, however. In 1843, Post wrote to Abby Kelley, an abolitionist Quaker who would also soon resign from the Society, that the overseers had "taken no further notice of my case," but she expected they would "have a fresh charge against me soon as I yesterday transcribed Epistles for the Preparative meetings" on paper which portrayed a slave in chains.[33]

Such acts of conscience had their price, however, and for women the payment again often appeared in familial terms. Thus, Amy must have wrestled with her choices for at least two more years, for in 1845 a letter from her mother, Mary Kirby, urged her to hold fast. "Lamentable indeed is the state of Society," she wrote as her daughter faced another inquiry from the Meeting for Sufferings. "I pity you," Mary Kirby continued, "but believe I might justly pity myself more and do sometimes look back [to] when I felt as an outcast from my friends. . . . Thou said thou would take no hasty steps. If I have any right to say, I desire you not to [and] hope you will overcome their evil with good."[34] By the end of the year, Amy had withdrawn from membership in the Genesee Yearly Meeting.

In the midst of the turmoil, more conservative Hicksite women began to use the powers gained for them by the dissidents. They did not falter, for instance, in disowning their offending sisters and did so without waiting upon the concurrence of the men's meeting. Here the powers gained by the women of the Genesee Yearly Meeting as a result of agitation by the most radical faction were now employed by more conservative female Friends to finalize their own departure. No wonder that some, like the Post women, chose to withdraw first.

Still, the use of these powers by conservative Hicksite women did not deter dissident female Friends from pushing for further change as a new discipline was established. Within the Yearly Meeting of Progressive Friends (first known as the Congregational Friends and later as the Friends of Human Progress), the separation of women's and men's meetings was abolished, marriage was performed without benefit of clerical or civic authority (and at least sometimes by women Friends themselves), the Meetings of Ministers and Elders and of Sufferings were abolished, and the two sexes were declared to have "common natures, common rights and a common destiny."[35]

Indeed, the entire "Basis of Religious Association" was predicated upon the absolute equality of persons, before God and on earth. The "Basis," moreover, emphasized collective action, proclaiming that women and men "are made pre-eminently social beings," and that from "the exercise of the social principles of our nature, flow all the reciprocal benefits." This concern with sociability may have originated in part from the restrictions previously imposed by Orthodox and Hicksite meetings of Quakers who mingled in worldly affairs. In their new association, Progressive Friends embraced all who accepted their principles and on an equal basis, "without limitation to sex, or complexion, or national peculiarities."[36]

It was from this fortified bastion of sex equality that Quaker women burst forth to secure rights for women in the larger society. When the Seneca Falls Woman's Rights meeting convened in July 1848, just a few weeks after the Progressive Quakers first gathered in nearby Farmington, feminist Friends led the charge for educational, economic, social, and political equity.[37] They continued the crusade in Rochester two weeks later and from there extended the campaign across the country and the century. Not only in New York but also in Ohio, Indiana, Michigan, and elsewhere in the Midwest, one could trace the emergence of grassroots women's rights movements to the pockets of Quaker upheaval.[38] In the years before the Civil War, female Friends constituted perhaps a quarter of all vocal woman's rights advocates; even afterward, they were the one religious denomination that was perpetually overrepresented among public agitators for sex equality.

What conclusion can we draw from these brief sketches of women's role in the Quaker schisms of the antebellum era? First, I would argue that the schisms of the 1820s and 1840s were not tragedies for women. This does not mean, however, that there were not painful moments of personal decision, such as those faced by Amy Post, her stepdaughter, and her sister as they proclaimed their "freedom from sectarian bondage" in the face of hesitation or outright opposition from husbands, mothers, sisters, and brothers. Nevertheless, the upheavals of the era allowed Amy Post and other female Friends to reassert their rights and powers in the ministry and meetings of the Hicksite and Progressive Friends and, for some, to assume real prominence alongside men.

It is possible that the divisions between Gurneyites and Wilburites also fostered women's reemergence as pillars of Quakerism. Ann Jones and Sarah Grubb led British Wilburites, with the latter reminding the men's meeting of London Yearly Meeting "to be steadfast in the truth and to uphold the standard of the faith."[39] Anna Braithwaite, another early crusader for Orthodoxy, now proclaimed in favor of Gurney's teachings, placing herself alongside Ester Wilkinson and Priscilla and Rachel Gurney, John Joseph Gurney's two preaching sisters.[40] Much more research is needed, however, before we can make any generalizations about women's roles in this period of Quaker upheaval.

What is clear is that in this as in every other period of division women arrayed themselves on both sides of the dispute. Neither more nor less progressive than their male brethren, women Friends were equally militant in opposing causes. Not a particular brand of theology or branch of Society was the key to women's participation. Rather upheaval itself seems to account for the emergence of strong-willed and outspoken women. That both Orthodox and Hicksite and later Hicksite and Progressive men railed against stubborn, emotional, and irrational women suggests the power that they perceived in their female opponents. On all sides, women seem to have sought greater deliberation, to have continued attempts at reconciliation longer, and to have recommended multiple investigations and inquiries more often than men. Once set upon a course, women often appeared more absolute in their determination to pursue the purest path.

However assertive, female Friends rarely voiced feminist sentiments. Their passion was not generally directed against their collective female condition nor toward its improvement. Indeed, Orthodox female Friends supported precisely those hierarchical structures and institutions that, in the long run, proved more detrimental to women's equality. Still, those women who supported first the Hicksite and later the Progressive Friends did augment their influence by agitating for a supportive brand of sectarian theology—one that emphasized the individual's relationship with God, the non-hierarchical character of religious societies, and the participation of the laity in policy-making positions.

The promotion of feminist reforms within the Society of Friends emerged gradually, hand in hand with proposals to limit the authority of ministers and elders and to allow "worldly" activity on behalf of abolitionism. Rules relating to marriage, to the discipline of female Friends, and to men's and women's concurrence on testimonies provided the wedge by which increasingly feminist-minded Friends promoted their cause. It is necessary, however, to analyze in greater detail the specific alterations in discipline and practice that appeared in various local meetings, particularly those relating to marriage, before we can determine women's success in achieving greater equality with men.[41] In addition, we need to explore men's support of these proposals for equality and to trace the kinship networks that often bound proponents of any one position together.

The significance of the drive for equality within the Society of Friends can only be fully comprehended within the context of economic, political, and social transformations in the world at large. The emergence of feminist Friends as opposed to non-feminist female leaders depended upon Quaker experiences in the antislavery movement and in the growing urban centers of western New York and the Midwest, which attracted increasing numbers of Quaker migrants. Feminist Friends need to be traced over two courses. First, by following the paths of Quaker migration we may be able to determine the geographical specificity of upheaval and female assertion.[42] Second, by following over time those Quaker women who first emerged as activists in the schism of 1828 and who two decades later appeared as agitators for woman's rights, we may be able to pinpoint the transformative experiences that caused particular female Friends to embrace or reject feminist politics.

Just as importantly, we need to continue our evaluation of feminist Friends' influence on the women's movement at large and, through that mass movement, on society as a whole. Both as national leaders and grassroots organizers, Quaker women were substantially overrepresented not only among early woman's rights advocates but also among abolitionists and pacifists. Many figures have already been reclaimed, particularly through the work of Margaret Hope Bacon, but much remains to be rediscovered. Specifically, we need more local studies of women's activities in the Hicksite and Progressive strongholds of the Midwest and rural Pennsylvania, and in the Gurneyite centers of New England.

Finally, just as women's historians have re-visioned the Renaissance, Enlightenment, French and American revolutions, and every other era and event where they have reclaimed women's experience, it is time to recast Quaker history. Though the fragmentation of Friends may have appeared a tragedy to men, both at the moment of division and in historical perspective; and though women and men may have suffered personal pain in the tumult of separation, the consequences for female Quakers may have been more positive than negative. After a decade of second thoughts, Amy Post finally declared in 1855 that she "greatly rejoiced in [her] freedom from sectarian bondage."[43]

As scholars and activists, perhaps we should rejoice, too. If upheaval that blurred the boundaries of women's role fostered female Quaker's activism, and if a strain of that activism then led to some Friends' advocacy of feminism, and if feminist Friends formed the core of the nineteenth-century woman's rights movement, and if that movement initiated transformations that began to reshape gender roles in more egalitarian ways, then the fragmentation of Friends was not a tragedy for Quaker women, but a triumph for us all. That is a prospect worth exploring.

NOTES

The author wishes to thank Drew Faust and Charles Rosenberg for providing encouragement and a quiet place to work at a critical moment in the writing of this essay.

1. Rufus M. Jones, *The Later Periods of Quakerism*, vol. 1 (1921; rpt., Westport, Conn.: Greenwood Press, 1970), 435.

2. H. Larry Ingle, *Quakers in Conflict: The Hicksite Reformation* (Knoxville: University of Tennessee Press, 1986), xiii.

3. Quote from Jones, *Later Periods*, 488, refers specifically to the years 1835 to 1855 but more generally to the entire period of schism from the 1820s through the 1850s.

4. Sherin Marshall Wyntjes, "Women in the Reformation Era," in Renata Bridenthal and Claudia Koonz, eds., *Becoming Visible: Women in European History* (Boston: Houghton Mifflin, 1977), 165.

5. Lyle Koehler, "The Case of the American Jezebels: Anne Hutchinson and Female Agitation during the Years of Antinomian Turmoil, 1636–1640," in Jean E. Friedman and William G. Shade, eds., *Our American Sisters: Women in American Life and Thought*, 3d ed. (Lexington, Mass: D. C. Heath, 1982), 19.

6. Keith Thomas, "Women and the Civil War Sects," *Past and Present* 13(April, 1958): 45. Phyllis Mack's study of Quaker women in this period provides a much more sophisticated and elaborate analysis of this phenomenon. See her "Gender and Spirituality in Early English Quakerism, 1650–1665" in this volume.

7. Quote from Wyntjes, "Women in the Reformation," 169; see also, Thomas, "Women and the Civil War Sects," 44.

8. Wyntjes, "Women in the Reformation," 187.

9. Here one cannot analyze women's advancement in the sects by either numbers of congregants or numbers of ministers. As with most religious denominations of the eighteenth and nineteenth centuries, women may have dominated Quakerism numerically. Still, this did not translate into women's active participation in the development of the sect's policies and programs except during periods of upheaval.

10. Jones, *Later Periods*, 32–33.

11. Jones, *Later Periods*, 129. See also, Margaret Hope Bacon, *Mothers of Feminism: The Story of Quaker Women in America* (San Francisco: Harper & Row, 1986), chps. 1–3.

12. Jones, *Later Periods*, 87–88.

13. Jones, *Later Periods*, 299, 283; and Bacon, *Mothers of Feminism*, 40–41, 78–79.

14. Rebecca Jones quoted in Bacon, *Mothers of Feminism*, 85.

15. Ingle, *Quakers in Conflict*, 117.

16. Ingle, *Quakers in Conflict*, 118–119.

17. Ingle, *Quakers in Conflict*, 126, 127–29.

18. Mary Willis to Amy Kirby, 182?, Isaac and Amy Post Family Papers, University of Rochester, Rochester, New York (hereafter cited as IAPFP). These papers provide dozens of letters discussing the Quaker schisms of the 1820s and 1840s. Other sets of family papers from other sections of the country must also be examined to determine the degree of involvement among women Friends who were not in the ministry and who were not elders but who participated in and actively discussed and analyzed the events of these years in private correspondence and in weekly, monthly, and quarterly meetings.

19. Material on the events at Green Street Monthly Meeting and its difficulties with Philadelphia Quarterly Meeting are from Ingle, *Quakers in Conflict*, 154–158, and 196–200.

20. On these events at the Green Street Meeting, see Ingle, *Quakers in Conflict*, 52, 207–208. Although Ingle is not analyzing women's roles separately from those of men, he does provide the material for doing so.

21. Poole quoted in Ingle, *Quakers in Conflict*, 163.

22. Ingle, *Quakers in Conflict*, 161, relates the events described in this paragraph.

23. Hannah Post to Amy Kirby, 29 January 1826, IAPFP.

24. Ingle, *Quakers in Conflict*, 51.

25. Quote from letter of John Ketcham to Isaac and Amy Post, 20 January 1829, IAPFP.

26. John Ketcham to Isaac and Amy Post, 20 January 1829, IAPFP.

27. Mary Robbins Post to Amy Post, October 183?, IAPFP. See also, Bacon, *Mothers of Feminism*, 93.

28. Sarah [Thayer] to Amy Post, 9 March 1853, IAPFP. By this time, Sarah Thayer had departed from the Hicksites, joined the Congregational or Progressive Friends, and adopted spiritualism.

29. For numerous examples, see Minutes, Rochester Monthly Meeting and Genesee Yearly Meeting, 1837 to 1848, Haviland Records Room, 15 Rutherford Place, New York, N. Y. 10003.

30. This quote from Hannah C. Greene to Amy Post, 17 May 1837, is one of several examples in the Isaac and Amy Post Family Papers.

31. See Nancy Hewitt, *Women's Activism and Social Change: Rochester, New York, 1822–1872* (Ithaca, N.Y.: Cornell University Press, 1984); "Amy Kirby Post," *The University of Rochester Library Bulletin*, 37 (1984): 5–21; and "Feminist Friends: Agrarian Quakers and the Emergence of Woman's Rights in America," *Feminist Studies* 12:1 (Spring 1986): 27–49. See also, Bacon, *Mothers of Feminism*, 91–97, on women's roles in the schisms of the 1820s, 1840s, and 1870s.

32. Lucy N. Colman, *Reminiscences* (Buffalo, N.Y.: H. L. Green, 1891), 84.

33. Amy Post to Abby Kelley, 4 December 1843, Abby Kelley Foster Papers, American Antiquarian Society, Worcester, Massachusetts.

34. M[ary R.] Kirby to Dear Daughters, 9 January 1845, IAPFP. See this volume.

35. Yearly Meeting of Congregational Friends, *Proceedings of the Yearly Meeting of Congregational Friends, Held at Waterloo, N.Y., from the Third to the Fifth of the Sixth Month, Inclusive, 1850* (Auburn, N.Y.: Henry Oliphant, Printer, 1850), 15. The reports from the annual meeting of the Congregational Friends/Progressive Friends/Friends of Human Progress in the years 1849 to 1861 provide numerous other examples.

36. See "Basis of Religious Association," in this volume.

37. Recognizing that the popular usage of the term *feminist* did not emerge in the United States until the early twentieth century, I nonetheless apply it to Progressive Quaker women in retrospect because I think that they captured, seventy years earlier, the "luxuriant growth" of woman's rights ideology described by Nancy Cott for the 1910s. On the definition and usage of the word *feminism*, see Nancy Cott, *The Grounding of Modern Feminism* (New Haven, Conn.: Yale University Press, 1987), introduction. Quote from p. 38.

38. See Hewitt, "Feminist Friends," and Bacon, *Mothers of Feminism*, chp. 7. See also the forthcoming book on the Seneca Falls Woman's Rights Convention of 1848 by Judith Wellman.

39. Quoted in Jones, *Later Periods*, 492–293. On the Gurneyite-Wilburite division, see the forthcoming dissertation, Brown University, on Rhode Island Quakers by Deborah VanBroekhoven.

40. Jones, *Later Periods*, 508–509.

41. Bacon, *Mothers of Feminism*, chp. 3, has demonstrated the potential of women's business meeting records to reveal important information about female Friends' struggle for equality within the Society. In chp. 5, Bacon suggests that some of the groundwork for equality between men and women, including educational equality, was laid during the nineteenth-century schisms.

42. Two studies that suggest the importance of midwestern meetings as centers for radical Quakerism are A. Day Bradley, "Progressive Friends in Michigan and New York," *Quaker History* 52 (1963): 95–103; and Carlisle G. Davidson, "A Profile of Hicksite Quakerism in Michigan, 1830–1860," *Quaker History* 59 (1970): 106–112.

43. Amy Post to Isaac Post, 14 June 1855, IAPFP.

DOCUMENTS

In January 1845, Mary Kirby of Jericho, Long Island, wrote to her daughters, Amy Kirby Post and Sarah Kirby Hallowell, in Rochester, New York. Mother Mary had agonized over divisions in the Society of Friends in the 1820s, and had apparently found herself isolated for a time from family and friends in the heat of that earlier schism. Now she saw her daughters facing a similar fate, one made more difficult by disagreement among her children (at least one of the sisters' siblings was entirely opposed to Quaker involvement in abolition) and by a series of family tragedies, including the death of Sarah's husband Jeffries Hallowell in the summer of 1844 and that of Amy and Isaac's infant daughter Maria Post a few months later. In addition, as age and illness advanced on friends and families, the contemplation of another upheaval in the Society must have especially saddened the elderly, who viewed meetings as a time to visit as well as worship, to gain solace from the circle of family and friends gathered together as the years slipped by.

Despite her mother's pleas, Amy Post withdrew from the Hicksite meeting before the year was through. Though she would eventually rejoice in the "freedom from sectarian bondage," in 1844–1845, personal loss, family tension, and spiritual disaffection coalesced in particularly dramatic and traumatic ways. Mary Kirby's letter captures this private side of the Quaker schisms.

The letter is reprinted by permission of the Department of Rare Books and Special Collections, University of Rochester Library. Spelling has been maintained from the original. Changes in capitalization and punctuation have been made only where it was necessary for clarity.

M[ary] Kirby to Dear Daughters, Jericho [Long Island], the 9th of First Month 1845.

Jericho the 9th of first Month 1845

Who would have thought 20 years ago that I should
be here to write this date 1845 but so it is, alas for
what—

Dear Daughters,

I have often mingled with you in sympathy in these deep tryals, no doubt they are permitd for some good purpose that is beyound our comprehension, and dear Amy I hope thou will endeavour to seek for resignation in thy keen tryal off thy darling and only little daughter, now in her lovely and inocent state, nothing to *mourn* for but our loss, hers is a shure and *Eternal Rest*. We knew of her beauty and loveliness, how like the rose so soon to drop and be gone, so will her sweetness remain, I trust, with many of us. We heard the affecting tidings by E. P. Willis' letter to PPW[1] but I said to myself my beloved Amy will not withhold her pen to us on so mournfull a theme, as the[e] know I always want to know more particular than he writes, but in this his feelings were very tenderly toucht. We had two of his letters to read, one before her exit.

Lamentable indeed is the state of society. I pity you, but believe I might more justly pity *myself* and do sometimes look back when I felt as an out cast from my friends, and am yet *as a nothing*. Thou said thou should take no hasty steps. If I have any right to say, I desire you not to. Hope you will overcome their evil with good. We have no new difficulties that I know. A very friendly intercourse seems to subsist, as to our Meetings business, perhaps in a few days, PPW and myself shall pay Hannah W. Underhill a vist on account of her uniting in marrage with a member, Jourdan Underhill, not acomplisht in the order of society.[2] Wilet comes in and says mother who [you] writing to. He sayt tell Amy to hold on going to meeting, not give it up, it looks so bad. They returned from their father Pettits yesterday, say the old folks are perty well, but their father seams at times to know but very little. John's wife Sally is poorly . . . perty much confined to the house. . . .

Lydia Seaman has made us a pleasant visit just before our Q[uarterly] Meeting, she seams perty comfortable but cannot come down stairs without some assistance, weekness in her back. At times I can hardly know how to realize it that Sister Sarah is gone, my husband and self visited her abought a week before her death. She said she had no pain, no not even a headache, her feet and legs very much swolen. I measured one just below the knee, it was over a half yard. She seamed very quiet and patient, so different from [what] she usually had been, she sat in her chair nights, had not laid down in 3 weeks, but she soon di[e]d after we left her. Seamed to sleep easy sitting. On Seventh day morning as Lydia was washing and dressing her feet which had both got soar, James was sitting by and said I believe she is gone, so easy, no apparent change. The corpse was brought up on the railroad second day morning—we met at the Mtg house at 2 o'clock, quite a number of friends came up with them. The corpse not exposed which was a tryal to her neighbors. . . .

And how does our dear Sarah feel, like being a resident with us? Our doors are open to receive the[e] cordially if their is no way that seams pleasenter to thee our beloved Sarah, but as to seaing any business that will be to thy advantage or satisfaction I seam as a blank.[3] I cant feel that I want thee to enter in our domestic affairs with very little gain (now don't feel that we don't want thee) *no entirely* otherways. I remarked Amy said scarse anything abought thee, I want to here from thee much more than we doe. . . .

[The letter continues with lengthy discussion of other visits, illnesses, and funerals]

My dear Jacob's health has been good all winter, no heavy cold, has not lost one meal from indisposition, mist only one meeting on account of snow drifts, cuts and saws wood for the franklin, eats a great many apples & reads hour after hour. This week very much engaged with Elwood's journal, last week the bible, sometimes the news paper takes his attention. Me head distress that I mentioned to you some time is very much [ ] and am comfortable. I most[ly] practice cold bathing every morning and conclude it has been beneficial. How is cousin A. Mo[tt], our love to her if you see her. Our Neighbours are now generaly in usual health. E W often over and cuts wood occasionally. . . . M W W has a tender feeling for you with much sympathy. Think to write ere its long.

I thought I would just say, Isaac has paid for the Standard long enuff for our folks.[4] I think they don't wish to pay it. Now you need never mention it on paper to us, to let our children know that I mentioned it to you.

fifth day morning, all well, in much love, M. Kirby Dear Children, it seams as tho I could not fold it up without desiring you to stand and wait patiently. it seams to me they will be overcome by your good and consistent lives. We can give you but a very limited account of our grandson Joseph Post.[5] Once and a while I see him at meeting, not been to see us but once since he commenced School.

[1]Edmund P. Willis was a cousin of Isaac Post's who would eventually marry the widowed Sarah Kirby Hallowell. Phebe Post Willis was an aunt to Isaac and Amy Post. She attended the Rochester Woman's Rights Convention, and the original minutes of that meeting are in the Phebe Post Willis Papers at the University of Rochester.

[2]Mary Kirby here refers to a committee of visitation from the Women's Monthly Meeting, which was generally responsible for assuring that marriages were performed according to the order of the Society. Amy and Isaac Post's marriage had come under investigation itself as a result of Amy being the sister of Isaac's first wife, Hannah Kirby.

[3]Sarah's husband Jeffries Hallowell had died unexpectedly and left his estate in deep debt. Sarah was therefore attempting to find some means of support. She would eventually remarry, and married and single she would dedicate increasing amounts of time to reform activities within the Society of Friends and in the world at large.

[4]Isaac Post often bought subscriptions to the *National Anti-Slavery Standard* and other abolitionist papers for family members. At least some of those for whom he paid on Long Island, including siblings of his and Amy's, rejected these attempts to be reformed.

⁵Joseph Post was the son of Isaac and Amy, who was sent to Long Island to attend school and to learn farming from his uncle. Amy periodically sent him antislavery literature and songbooks, temperance pledges, and other reminders of his Rochester family's dedication to reform.

The "Basis of Religious Association" is a set of principles adopted by those reform-minded Quakers who left the Genesee Yearly Meeting of (Hicksite) Friends in June 1848. Gathering as soon as the Genesee Meeting rejected any chance of reforming Quaker discipline from within, the dissidents met in Farmington, New York, to discuss plans for forming a new religious society. They agreed to meet again in October in Waterloo, in the meantime encouraging other activists to join their ranks and drafting a set of principles for consideration by the body as a whole. In the intervening months, a number of these new Congregational Friends participated in the founding of the woman's rights movement at Seneca Falls, New York. Four of the dissidents, Amy Post, Mary Hallowell, Sarah Fish, and Rhoda DeGarmo, also served on the committee of arrangements for the Rochester Woman's Rights Convention held two weeks later. Thus, it is not surprising that the "Basis" agreed upon at Waterloo in October proclaimed complete equality for women as well as for blacks, Indians, and all other social groups. Adopted by circles of dissident Quakers in Michigan, Pennsylvania, Ohio, Indiana, and across New York State, the "Basis" knit together a loose but extensive community of activists. Through annual meetings (held at least until 1861 in upstate New York), pamphlets, speakers, and local gatherings, these Congregational, or Progressive, Friends labored for spiritual and earthly equality for all women and men.

This document can be found in the Quaker Collection at Haverford College.

Basis of Religious Association

Adopted by the Conference held at Farmington, in the State of New York, on the Sixth and Seventh of Tenth month, 1848

To all to whom these may come.
Beloved Brethren and Sisters:

Having, pursuant to adjournment in the 6th month last, again met, to consider what measure it will be right to adopt, that the blessings of Religious Society may be placed within the reach of all, our minds have been led into an examination of religious association in general. In looking at this subject, melancholy evidences present on every hand, that societies or church organizations, ostensibly for the promotion of religion, have been among the greatest impediments to its progress, and the most fruitful sources of tyranny and oppression. But, while we feel that these facts should lead to the utmost care in regard to the principles permitted to enter into their structure, we are abundantly assured that these results are their abuse, not their necessary attendants—the consequence of the admission into them of elements hostile to man's nature, his duties, and inalienable rights.

Religious association has manifestly its foundation in the religious and social elements of the human mind—principles powerful and constant in our nature, and most beneficent in their legitimate action. We are made pre-eminently social beings. From the exercise of the social principles of our nature, flow all the reciprocal benefits, all the countless offices of love and kindness, which strew with blessings the path of life. Not only in the physical, but especially in the higher departments of man's nature—the moral and religious— we behold the working of this beautiful and beneficent economy; in the mingling of sympathies and affections; in imparting to each other the treasures of the intellect, the conscience, the religious feelings; in united aspirations to, and reverence and adoration of, the Supreme Being.

To attain these social religious benefits in the highest degree, assemblies are needed; these require arrangement, time, manner, as well as object; in short, organization, or understood modes of action. We need only that these be wise and right—not conflicting with man's prerogatives, nor God's.

The object of religious association may be defined in brief to be, the promotion of righteousness—of practical goodness—love to God and man—on the part of every member composing the association, and in the world at large. So far as it is instrumental to this end, it is Christian, a blessing to the community in which it exists. So far as it is not thus instrumental, its non-existence were desirable. To promote this object there must be a practical conformity to the Divine laws—the principles of the association must be in harmony with the principles of the Divine government. For righteousness is none other than the result of these laws—the exemplification of these principles in the actions of moral agents.

Man is made to sustain a relation of an intelligent and accountable agent under the Supreme Intelligence; has the law of God
written on the conscious powers of his soul; stands in such con-
tiguity to Omnipresent God as to have immediately revealed to
him God's will regarding him. THIS IS THE FUNDAMENTAL
FACT IN RELIGION; that which constitutes man a subject of
God's moral government; the foundation of his hopes, of his accountability. This revelation of God's will to him he feels and
knows to be personal—his accountability personal and not transferable, though connecting him in obligation, and binding him by
kindred ties with the whole family of man. Yet, as absolutely personal and individual as though he and God were alone in the Universe. Hence his conscience must be kept sacred in it, devotion and
allegiance to God, from whom the law comes. No laws nor institutions of men, should restrict this individual exercise of conscience,
of responsibility. The only restriction that can be Christian or law-
ful in this momentous matter, in the terms of association, is the
admission of the obvious principle, that no pretext of conscience
can be valid which violates the equal rights of others, or any of the
unchangeable principles of moral obligation, which are primary to
conscience, and by which, in the Divine order, it is to be governed.

Liberty of conscience, then—the recognition of the right of every member to act in obedience to the evidence of Divine Light, in
its present and progressive unfoldings of truth and duty to the
mind, must be a fundamental principle in every right organization.
That this perfect liberty of conscience, is the right of every sane and
accountable human being, appears from several other consider-
ations. Mankind partake of the variety which every where marks
the Creator's works. Though identical in the elements of their
being, these elements exist in the race in infinitely diversified pro-
portions. Hence their individuality, their peculiarities of character.
Again: they are each subject to influences as diversified as their
mental and physical peculiarities—all which affect their character,
their views, their actions. This diversity furnishes occasion for a
most profitable exercise of some of the finest feelings and affections
of our nature—tenderness, kindness, tolerance. From the universal-
ity of the facts in the case, the practice of these virtues is obligatory
on all, and no institution can be Christian—can exemplify love to

God and man—(the substance of Christianity)—that is deficient in these virtues. "Christianity," says an enlightened writer, "respects this diversity in men—aiming not to undo but further God's will; not fashioning all men after one pattern—to think alike, act alike, be alike, even look alike. It is something far other than Christianity which demands that. A Christian church then should put no fetters on the man; it should have unity of purpose, but with the most entire freedom for the individual. When you sacrifice the man to the mass in church or state—church or state becomes an offence, a stumbling-block in the way of progress, and must end or mend. The greater the varitey of individualities in church or state, the better is it—so long as all are really manly, humane, and accordant. A Church must needs be partial, not catholic, where all men think alike—narrow and little." It has been the want of this broad and Christian ground of toleration that has been the bane of every church, Catholic and Protestant. In proportion to its absence, despotic and oppressive measures have marred the harmony and painfully defeated the objects of religious society.

Another cause of the exercise of despotic power in professed Christian churches, has been the establishment of an ascending scale of authority of larger bodies over smaller, terminating in a Head of Supreme Controlling Power. This, we are persuaded, has been a prominent cause of the difficulties which have been experienced in the Society of Friends, at different periods of its history, and especially of the divisions which have occurred within the last quarter of a century.

In the establishment of Preparative, Monthly, Quarterly, and Yearly Meetings, it was, doubtless, not contemplated, in the early periods of the Society, that any despotic authority should be exercised by larger meetings over smaller. The only power intended to be exercised, appears to have been that of persuasion and love. But the history of the Society shows how easy it is to abuse power, when men have incautiously been vested with it, by the expressed or implied rules of a written code. And the experience of the past admonishes us to recur to original fundamental ground, in regard to the design of religious association, and remove from it an element demonstrably evil in its tendency and results—*the subordination of meetings,* or the vesting of larger meetings with authority over smaller. As in a right organization the man cannot be sacrificed to the mass, the individual conscience to an assemblage of consciences; so neither can a number of individual consciences in a congregation rightfully be sacrificed to a larger assembly, or any assumed or established head. The order of independent congregations therefore, has opened, with great unanimity and clearness, as most in harmony with man's nature and rights, and least liable to abuse.

Each congregation or meeting, will consequently attend to its own internal or disciplinary concerns. Larger meetings—Quarterly or Yearly—will be for *counsel and advice,* and for the consideration and promotion of the great interests of humanity—everything that concerns man at large—including of consequence the removal of the existing evils of the day, War, Slavery, Intemperance, Licentiousness, or in whatever form cruelty, injustice, and other perverted principles may operate. Yearly meetings may suggest rules or regulations for the government of particular meetings or congregations, but shall have no power to enforce.

Another fruitful cause of difficulty and disaffection, has been the institution of Meetings of Ministers and Elders. Of these we propose the discontinuance, as also of the practice of recommending or ordaining ministers. Every meeting or congregation will attend to the regulation of the ministry among themselves: and if any one proposing to travel to a distance, wishes a certificate of moral character, it can be granted for the time being.

Not only will the equality of woman be recognized, but so perfectly, that in our meetings, larger and smaller, men and women will meet together and transact business jointly.

These principles, simply carried out, will, we apprehend, effectually prevent the abuses and evils of ecclesiastical organizations. And should they at any time fail to be exemplified in the practice of a meeting toward any of its members, the evil would be limited, and not very oppressive, as any member affected by it, would be at liberty to join another congregation, and still participate in the privileges of the general association.

Two evils at least, if not wholly excluded, would find but scanty soil to grow in—*Tyranny and Sectarianism.* And these will be the more effectually prevented by the recognition of the great principle, already adverted to, of perfect liberty of conscience—which, in our view, forbids the establishing of any thing as a barrier to religious fellowship, either as regards individuals or the inter-communication of congregations, but the violation of the great unchangeable principles of morals, revealed, as facts of consciousness, to the universal human mind—Reverence of God, Justice, Mercy, Benevolence, Veracity, Chastity, &c. In other words, nothing but what is plainly incompatible with *love to God,* and *love to man*—leaving each to the test: "By their fruits ye shall know them," independently of abstract opinions. Thus a brother or sister might hold the doctrine of the Trinity, or of a Vicarious Atonement—might practice Water Baptism, the ceremony of Bread and Wine, and kindred rituals, or he might believe none of these, and his right should be recognized to preach his conscientious convictions of these matters in any of our meetings—each, in either case, conceding the right of every other brother and sister, who may deem that error has been promulgated, to endeavor, in the pure spirit of love and kindness, to make it apparent, either before the same congregation, or in any of our meetings where they apprehend themselves called upon to do so. Thus, by the recognition of equal rights, and the sacredness of conscience, and of the duty of reciprocal kindness, a narrow sectarianism and party feeling would vanish before the light of truth, and the minds of the sincere and pious be more and more united. Nothing would be found so potent to promote unanimity of sentiment and brotherly love, as action based on these Divine principles. Under their influence a censorious and contentious spirit would find no place, the governing desire would be the attainment of truth. And thus would be verified the words of the excellent Isaac Penington— "It is not the different practice from one another that breaks the peace and unity, but the judging one another because of differing practices."

We may advert to yet another great evil, which, in the church order we have defined, must receive an effectual check. We mean *Priestcraft.* This naturally grows out of a dependence on our fellow beings, as possessing superior means of Divine knowledge. In this dependence individual talents are neglected, and individual responsibility is sought to be transferred to the person or persons on whom the dependence rests. And this dependence gives POWER to those on whom it is placed, and makes those who place it easy subjects for its exercise. In this way a large proportion of the professors of religion become, to a greater or less extend, the dupes of priestcraft. The same effect takes place, to a certain extent, among Friends, as the consequence of *recommending ministers,* as it is called; that is, setting them apart, by a particular process, as ministers of the Society. By this practice—which is a virtual ordination—the idea naturally obtains that those thus distinguished have nearer access to the Divine Mind—superior means of Divine knowledge, than others. This leads to an improper dependence on them, and a consequent neglect on the part of the other members of their own spiritual gifts. Here great injury is sustained, both by the preachers and those who thus defer to them; and by the non-employment of individual gifts, in the inculcation of moral and religious truth, the body and community at large suffer inculculable loss.

Intimately connected with the right use of the gifts of every member, is the mode of conducting assemblies for spiritual edification and improvement—of which we will here say a word. Agreeably to the facts before stated, and the objects of religious association, every accountable human being stands in such a relation to the Divine Mind, as to be privileged to receive, from the Fountain of Wisdom and Goodness, immediate instruction relative to all the duties of life, personal and social. The responsibility in respect to these duties being personal, and not transferable, no one can appoint another to act for him in their fulfillment. Fidelity to God can be maintained only by individual obedience to Divine requiring. No society arrangement can be right, which admits not of this obedience. No man has a right to absolve himself from it. In view of these important truths, we deem that a true church organization does not admit of placing one or more persons over a congregation as the stated spiritual teacher, or teachers. Consistently with individual rights and responsibilities, we must meet together as brethren, recognizing one Divine Teacher, and leaving the mind of each free, to speak or be silent, according to his highest perceptions of duty, and in agreement with a just estimate of each other's equal rights. Thus may the gifts of all be exercised in the promotion of truth and goodness, and while they are improved "by reason of use," the body will "edify itself in love."

Associating on these principles, we have concluded to hold Yearly Meeting, in Friends' Meeting-House, known as Junius, (now Waterloo,) Seneca County, New York, commencing on Second-day, the 4th of 6th month next, 1849, at 11 o'clock in the morning: and we recommend that Friends, in their different meetings, who may be prepared for the measure, appoint representatives accordingly. And we further invite all, of whatever name or wherever scattered, who unite in the principles of the foregoing basis of association, to be present and participate with us in the objects contemplated—to promote truth, piety, righteousness, and peace in the earth. That all may find in the endearments of Religious Society a HOME for their spirits, and that, by a union of effort, virtue and happiness may be diffused in the human family, and God be glorified, who is over all, blessed forever.

Signed on behalf of the Conference.

Thomas M'Clintock,
Rhoda De Garmo, Clerks

Proceedings of the Yearly Meeting of Congregational Friends, held at Waterloo, New York. From the 4th to the 6th of Sixth Month, inclusive, 1849. Auburn: Oliphant's Press, 1849.

FOUR

The Twentieth Century

BARBARA MILLER SOLOMON

Dilemmas of Pacifist Women, Quakers and Others, in World Wars I and II

IN THE FIRST half of the twentieth century, American women became a dominant force in the peace movement. While willingly joining male-led groups women had greater impact when they formed separate organizations. Quakers and non-Quakers contributed to the spectrum of diverse pacifist attitudes. Pacifists acting to influence American foreign policy discovered that commitments to the principle of peace created daunting moral dilemmas. From the onset of World War I to the end of World War II, individuals and groups of different backgrounds sought to reconcile opposition to war with loyalties to country, their own sex, ethnic and religious ties, and to humanity. Unpredictable world events challenged pacifist goals and changed the issues over time. Reformers faced the onset and actuality of the first world war, then continued through the postwar reaction to a time of positive engagement for peace efforts in the 1920s and early 1930s only to encounter the new challenges from the fascist and Nazi threats that engulfed the globe in a second war. Women and men responded in divergent ways to their conflicts of conscience amid changing circumstances. This essay focuses on the dilemmas of Quaker women and their influence as leaders in the secular groups they formed in association with non-Quakers.[1]

While advocacy of peace is a common religious aspiration, the Quaker faith provides a central place for the specific testimony against the world's ills. For the historian, the Quaker process of testifying for peace provides a framework for understanding and interpreting dilemmas of reformers and the different conclusions they reach. Bear in mind that witnessing for peace is only one of several testimonies a Quaker may choose; other testimonies address religious, social, and racial forms of oppression. When dilemmas arise because one testimony conflicts with another in specific circumstances, Quakers rely on a distinctive consensual process that enables an individual to acknowledge conflicts of conscience. Other Quakers give support to the individual's struggle and resolution of the dilemma over choices, whether or not they are in agreement with the outcome. When this consensual process succeeds, it leads to a higher stage of resolution.[2]

While pacifist dilemmas existed before the twentieth century, the peace testimony has had greater impact in the era of global war. By the same token, secular pacifist organizations took root slowly in the nineteenth century. Organized pacifism had its beginnings in the American Peace Society of 1828, which collapsed over the divisive issue of the Civil War. Yet soon thereafter, in 1866, the Universal Peace Union was formed. Women as well as men joined these organizations, but the female presence was limited and did not influence leadership. These societies emphasized peaceful solutions through arbitration and use of international law.[3]

Portents of women's future work for peace emerged when in 1872 Quaker feminist Lucretia Mott, one of the authors of the 1848 Seneca Falls Declaration of Sentiments for women's rights, determined to devote the rest of her life to peace organizing. Similarly, at this time Unitarian suffragist Julia Ward Howe, author of the "Battle Hymn of the Republic," placed work for peace above all causes. In 1887, Frances Willard established the Department of Peace and Arbitration of the Women's Christian Temperance Union, with Hannah Bailey, a Maine Quaker, in charge. Finally, at the turn of the century, the Spanish-American War evoked conspicuous anti-imperialist protests from religious-minded pacifists and other intellectuals.[4]

For women, momentum for peace reform accompanied the growing suffrage activism. In Boston, Unitarian author and lecturer Lucia Ames Mead (wife of Edwin Mead, a well-known peace leader) stimulated fellow suffragist Fannie Fern Andrews to found the American School Peace League in 1908; by 1915 there were forty branches. Prophetically, in 1909 a future secular leader, Hannah Clothier Hull, not only represented the Women's Yearly Meeting, but also the entire Yearly Meeting of the Philadelphia Hicksites at a peace conference of Quakers.[5]

Support for pacifist ideals increased with each decade. The first significant widening of controversial peace activism occurred with the outbreak of European war in August 1914. This event stunned people everywhere. In the United States, a broad range of professional men and women—reform-minded conservatives, liberals, and radicals—all competed for control of the peace movement. Social workers, journalists, academics, and religious leaders reacted to the crisis by calling meetings and forming groups to work for an early peace. One such meeting of men and women at the Henry Street Settlement in New York City resulted in the founding of the American Union Against Militarism. Quakers and other religious leaders formed the radical Fellowship of Reconciliation at that time. Among the various women's groups, the Woman's Peace Party proved the most important over time in reaching women. With dramatic and far-reaching consequences, Jane Addams, head of the Woman's Peace Party in 1915, persuaded leading American professional women to accept the invitation of their European counterparts to meet at The Hague to consider ways to bring the war to an early end. The deliberations of the participants led to the founding after the war of the Women's International League for Peace and Freedom (WILPF).[6]

Despite the public efforts of pacifist Americans, Woodrow Wilson declared war in 1917, and pacifism became unpatriotic. Wartime regulations brought critical dilemmas for those Americans who continued their pacifist opposition. Protest increasingly verged on illegality or became overtly illegal. Patriotism seemed to require repression of free speech against the war.

Only a small minority of women and a few men refused to subside. Activists in marginal groups, which generally included women and men, persisted. Among these were the Bureau of Legal First Aid (1917–1920), operated by Frances Witherspoon and Tracy Mygatt, young Bryn Mawr graduates; the Anti-Enlistment League, founded by Jessie Wallace Hughan; and the Women's Peace Party of New York, headed by Crystal Eastman. The American Union Against Militarism (AUAM) continued and new coalitions formed, including the Emergency Peace Federation (EPF) and the People's Council (PC). Radical women participated with radical men: Christian socialists and Marxist socialists together. Members of such groups were usually absolute pacifists, and significantly, the women were usually feminists.[7]

Jane Addams and other Hull House leaders, as well as Wellesley professor Emily Greene Balch, stayed uneasily on the side of radical antiwar youth groups. But for most Americans who joined the war effort, tolerance of protestors disappeared. The remnant of pacifists, Balch included, still tried to influence public opinion through the press, lectures, parades, and mass meetings. While American participation in the war was short, nineteen months ending 11 November 1918, protestors paid a price. Several academic men lost their jobs—and one woman, Professor Balch of Wellesley College. Some men, including Eugene Debs, went to prison. Jane Addams's popularity waned.

Some men and women in their trials of conscience found a needed solace in religion, and Quakers were ready to give them support. Emily Balch, deeply religious all her life, had informed the Wellesley trustees that she could not support the war because

I believe so deeply that the way of war is not the way of Christianity. I find it so impossible to reconcile war with the truths of Jesus' teaching, that even now I am obliged to give up the happiness of full and unquestioned cooperation where the responsibility of choice is mine.[8]

During the war, Balch, along with others, joined the Fellowship of Reconciliation; she was well on her way to becoming a Quaker. Already a visible advocate for peace, Balch was drawn to being a convinced Quaker by the communion she witnessed in Friends' meetings.[9]

If for a minority of pacifists religious faith strengthened the will to protest against the war, feminism by contrast more often offered an argument for peace reformers to give support to the war. Those who had joined suffrage organizations developed political consciousness even before they could vote and already looked to a future in which women would share in making a better, more peaceful world. For many, the old connection between feminist and pacifist consciousness operated differently once the United States was at war. They did not give priority to feminism and pacifism for the immediate time. Moreover, feminist consciousness, while apparently subdued, still had credence in their decision to give strong support to the war. With the Nineteenth Amendment still three years away in 1917, suffragists agreed with two activists of different generations, Carrie Chapman Catt and Harriot Stanton Blatch, to drop pacifist stands. Implicit in their thinking was the importance of showing female loyalty to country and proving that women were worthy of the vote. Thus, in 1917 commitment to peace might or might not yield to commitment to equality of the sexes, and both were compellingly challenged by commitment to patriotism. [10]

But one woman leader reacting differently, held her own ground. Alice Paul, Quaker-born and raised, took a stand that was hard for both feminists and pacifists to justify. As the head of the National Woman's Party (NWP), she made a conscious decision to remove herself both from the activism of women's organizations and from the participation of other women in the war effort. Always an extermist, Paul made her position clear in the last suffrage protests during the war: seeking equality of women would remain her sole political objective. Quaker-educated at Swarthmore College, Paul made feminism, not pacifism, an abiding commitment. If I may use Quaker terms, Paul had chosen one testimony, that for women's equality. She faced no conflicts.

Yet, Alice Paul's thinking was not simple in her advice to Jeannette Rankin, who encountered a special personal and public dilemma as the first woman elected to the U.S. House of Representatives. Should she vote against President Wilson's Declaration of War in April 1917? Paul told Rankin that in the Woman's Party there were individual members in the suffrage picket line who supported the war and others who opposed it. Nonetheless Alice Paul told Jeanette Rankin that

it would be a tragedy for the first woman ever in Congress to vote for war. That the one thing that seemed to us so clear was that women were the peace-loving half of the world and that by giving power to women we would diminish the possibilities of war. [11]

Nonetheless Alice Paul refused personally to participate either in peace or war efforts. She stated that until women had equality with men she would not deviate from the cause of feminism. Paul shocked pacifists, yet her view was not inconsistent with her Quaker membership. In the Quaker idiom, Paul chose public testimony for equality of women, even though she believed, abstractly, in pacifism.

The connections between pacifism and feminism remained complex and strained after World War I. Near the end of her life, Alice Paul recalled Jane Addams's urging her at "our final [post-suffrage] convention" (15 February 1921) to "just merge in with the WILPF." Although Paul admitted that many of the members of the National Woman's Party wanted to participate in the peace movement, she was not ready to relinquish the cause of women's equality. Those who proposed that the NWP make world disarmament its new goal were defeated at the convention.[12]

Yet Jane Addams was prescient. In the 1920s, many who shared in the triumph of suffrage were ready to make the cause of peace central. The plethora of peace groups multiplying in the decade stemmed from a strong sense among Americans that another world war must never be allowed.

When I was growing up in Boston in the 1920s and 1930s, I learned at home, at school, and at Sunday school that war was the overriding evil that must never occur again. My father, whose brother had been killed in France just before the Armistice, expressed relief that I was a girl who would not be "cannon fodder." It is evident that my teachers felt much the same way and transmitted the horrors of war to their pupils at every opportunity.

Today, as a historian I see the links between my education and the women's peace organizations that promoted peace by providing books, pamphlets, radio talks, and the like to strengthen the public climate of opinion toward a permanent peace. Those women's groups believed that the younger generation, if properly enlightened, would prevent the United States from ever joining again in a European war. What I and others imbibed reflected the rising influence of the peace movement.

The 1920s peace groups envisaged the shaping of public opinion as an important means of preventing wars, and therefore they promoted peace education in schools as well as churches. For adult education, peace organizations furthered the study of conflicts among nations with attention to economic and social factors that explain different viewpoints and behavior of nations. Discussions included treatment of enemies, especially of women and children. Also, peace advocates believed that meetings with representatives of other countries were needed to encourage international understanding. These undertakings were liberal approaches to the prevention of war, favored by pacifists, both Quaker and non-Quaker men and women.

Before treating the best-known organization, the Quaker-inspired Women's International League for Peace and Freedom, it is important to view the other contemporary associations, for the sheer volume of them makes plain that the promotion of peace in the decade after World War I was in vogue among educated women of varied backgrounds. In a 1929 article "Women in International Affairs," feminist-pacifist Florence Brewer Boeckel listed numerous women's organizations that were concerned with international affairs and dealt either implicitly or explicitly with questions of war and peace. Some were formed through religious affiliations that attracted particular memberships. Others represented an array of organizations whose concerns were not focused solely on peace but on various reforms or professional interests.[13]

Those with an exclusive focus on peace included the Women's Council for Education in International Relations, the Women's Peace Union, the Women's Peace Society, and the Women's International league for Peace and Freedom. Such organizations usually started in the Northeast and spread. What was also significant in Boeckel's survey was the marked growth of organizations that were international in membership: the International Alliance of Women for Suffrage and Equal Citizenship, the World Woman's Christian Temperance Union, the World Young Women's Christian Association, the International Association of University Women, and the World Union of Women.[14]

The expansion of women's organizations in the 1920s and 1930s showed the staying power of separate female voluntary associations. Certain peace leaders still believed that women were more effective operating outside male-dominated associations in conveying women's presumedly different values on public issues. Boeckel could not state the total membership in these organizations but believed it stood in the millions. Nor did she mention the women members in the more than one hundred peace organizations in the United States that were mixed in membership, although largely male and certainly directed by men.

In one sense, that of public interest, the peace cause between the two world wars represented mass opinion; but in a stricter sense it never became an effective mass movement. Only one peace organization, the WILPF, at times contained sufficient numbers to constitute a critical mass. Even in the WILPF, while leaders and members expressed a spectrum of views, it was mainly the leadership that was politicized and in control of its activities.

Why were there so many peace organizations? I suggest that different groups served constituencies not for the peace issue alone, but for political or religious platforms as well. Moreover, individuals worked for peace within groups in which they felt socially comfortable.[15]

The overlap in membership among these women's groups is instructive as well. For example, several officers of the Women's Committee for World Disarmament, including Florence Brewer Boeckel, were active in the National Woman's Party. The available choices for peace membership ranged from Carrie Chapman Catt's conservative National Committee on the Cause and Cure of War (1925) to the radical Women's Peace Society established by Fanny Garrison Villard and the Women's Peace Union founded by the initiative of Canadian Christine Ross Barker. Finally, the most consequential in longevity and influence was the Women's International League for Peace and Freedom.[16]

Catt's National Committee, an umbrella organization for the American Association of University Women, the General Federation of Business and Professional Women's Clubs, the National League of Women Voters, and the National Women's Christian Temperance Union, stayed within the bounds of peace policies approved by the United States government. By contrast, the Women's Peace Society and the Women's Peace Union both upheld the radical principle of absolute nonresistance. In addition, the Women's Peace Union campaigned for a constitutional amendment to make it illegal for the United States to wage war.

Unlike most of these other groups, the WILPF was not rigidly monolithic in its stands. Retrospectively in 1979, a former lobby-ist, Dorothy Detzer, explained that the WILPF's membership in-cluded three main groups. First, "[t]he majority . . . followed the leadership of Miss Addams and Miss Balch. They actively sup-ported the policies formulated at the Annual meetings of the League and the programs to implement those policies thru [*sic*] political undertakings." Next in Detzer's formulation came a mi-nority group, followers of Alice Paul, who wanted the orga-nization to support the Equal Rights Amendment. These women appeared to emphasize freedom above peace. Third, Detzer identi-fied another minority, a smaller group, who were nonresisters, "absolutists" in the cause of peace. They were unwilling to accept much of Detzer's lobbying, objecting, for example, to the league's refusal to demand "the immediate abolition of the army and navy" at congressional hearings.

How does the historian reconcile the different perceptions and assessments of the WILPF? The league's range of members from moderate to extremist in the means they would employ to achieve the agreed-on end of peace precipitated varied public judgments. Overall the WILPF was always associated with liberalism and radi-calism of one kind or another.[17]

In the 1920s, disagreements among the pacifist groups abounded in both the external and internal spheres. After World War I, reac-tionary fears in the United States government made virtually *all* women's groups suspect, except the Daughters of the American Revolution (DAR). The WILPF was conspicuous in lobbying against political candidates who supported larger military appro-priations in peacetime. But it was not alone in becoming a target of political observers from the right, the middle, and the left for the efforts of a whole range of women's groups to reduce military spending, to oppose chemical warfare, and to call for total disarma-ment. Press attention stimulated paranoid accusations against all women's groups.

Even the cautious peace organization of Carrie Chapman Catt, the National Committee on the Cause and Cure of War, was at-tacked by the War Department, specifically by Brigadier General Amos A. Fries of its Chemical Warfare Service. Under his direc-tion, a staff collected information designating as subversive fifteen women's organizations and twenty-nine women leaders. From his investigations, the notorious Spider Web chart was produced in 1923, purportedly uncovering an "interlocking directorate of women's organizations" whose Bolshevik tendencies represented an attack on the United States government. The Spider Web included affiliates of the liberal establishment lobby, the Women's Joint Congressional Committee (WJCC), that is, the League of Women Voters, the Women's Christian Temperance Union, and many others. The WILPF was clearly branded as socialistic and Bolshevistic, and Jane Addams, among others, was singled out for condemnation. The public damage was not easily erased, but committed women activists were not deterred.[18]

Among the most staunch groups was the WILPF with its conspicuously Quaker leadership. However, the organization was never defined through the religious affiliation of the members nor was the leadership exclusively Quaker. Rather, the WILPF matured between the two world wars under the direction of women who were either active Quakers or "Quaker-related," to use Margaret Bacon's apt term. Settlement leader Jane Addams of Hull House had Quaker parentage but joined the Episcopal church. Emily Greene Balch was a Quaker by conviction, and Hannah Clothier Hull, equally firm, was a birthright Quaker. After losing her Wellesley professorship, Balch developed a second career in the WILPF; it became the base through which she conducted research investigations, with her reports circulating to governments as well as to the WILPF membership. After serving as paid international secretary-treasurer (1919–1922), she held many posts, succeeding Jane Addams as president of the U.S. section (1931) and as honorary international president (1937). She played a critical role in the WILPF's policy making.

Mildred Scott Olmsted, not Quaker-born but in time a convinced Friend, became interested in the WILPF in the 1920s. She had served during World War I first with the military forces in France under the auspices of the YMCA, and thereafter joined the American Friends Service Committee in relief work with starving children in Germany. From 1935 to 1966, Olmsted served as national executive secretary of the U.S. section of the WILPF. Similarly Dorothy Detzer, the WILPF's most effective lobbyist, had worked at Quaker missions in both Austria and Russia in the early 1920s. Detzer, without becoming a Quaker, learned to appreciate Quaker approaches to mediating disagreements.[19]

Undoubtedly the U.S. section of the WILPF benefited from the Quaker mode of mediating differences. This method of listening to different points of view before resolving differences through a consensus was introduced by Jane Addams and later it was reinforced by Emily Greene Balch, Hannah Clothier Hull, Mildred Scott Olmsted, and others. These individuals were accustomed to mediation that was integral to the religious meetings of Quakers who understood that different persons had different convictions on particular matters; it was expected that the whole meeting would absorb, consider, and resolve differences presented to the body of worshippers. Thus, the Quaker-trained or experienced participating in secular groups had the discipline to withstand criticism even when it was unwarranted.[20]

Leaders of the WILPF expected hostile attacks during World War I, but in the 1920s the league was officially isolated from the major establishment organizations. These included the Women's Joint Congressional Committee and the Committee on the Cause and Cure of War, even though some WILPF members did belong to specific groups within these two coalitions. Not only did the WILPF have to cope with conservative and liberal groups who sought to distance themselves, but it had also to deal with criticism from the National Woman's Party that the WILPF was not radical enough on feminist issues![21]

Many preserved observations and judgments about the WILPF stem from the vested interests of peace participants. On the whole, their comments ignore the fact that all the women's peace groups managed to cooperate in public events for disarmament. Despite the rivalries of their societies, the women activists marched together in peace parades, supported each other's lobbying, and took common satisfaction in the ratification of the Kellogg-Briand Peace Pact by the U. S. Congress in 1928. Moreover, the women's organizations also collaborated with men's groups. The WILPF, for example, was one of the original members of the National Council for the Prevention of War, a clearinghouse for peace groups with Quaker Frederick Libby as its executive secretary. By the 1930s, the U.S. WILPF had organized peace councils in local communities in which a variety of men's and women's organizations worked cooperatively.[22]

Internal tensions in the various women's groups reflected in part generational differences. Older activists were more often single women, while some younger ones were trying to combine marriage and career or, if single, were viewed as less sober or "in the flapper mode." One would like to know whether the WILPF or other women's peace groups attracted any collegians in the 1930s. Undergraduates of both sexes who became peace activists had other options of course. They could either join purely political leftist organizations like the American Student Union or serve with the Friends Service Committee founded in 1917.[23]

That some American WILPF members were accustomed to and even preferred working with men rather than separately is suggested by an incident at the Zurich Conference in 1934. At that meeting, Mildred Scott Olmsted moved that the WILPF's constitution be amended to include men as well as women and that an appropriate name change be effected. But the motion was withdrawn in part because of the opposition of the European branches. There the feeling persisted that it was worthwhile for women to continue their separate organizations where "different" female views would prevail.[24]

Despite unfavorable publicity, the WILPF membership in the U.S. section grew in the 1920s and 1930s. The initial 52 members expanded to 1100 by 1921 and then to 9514 by 1930. While figures for the mid-1930s fluctuate between 13,000 and 16,000, the membership of 13,000 in 1940 reduced swiftly to 11,500 by January 1941. The WILPF's tolerance for different views in the membership extended to other groups, from National Woman's Party feminists (who often joined the WILPF) to establishment liberal supporters to absolute pacifists.[25]

Importantly, throughout its history the WILPF was an international body and European sections kept alive the ideal of an international order. The U.S. section was successful in pursuing research and in sending groups on missions to other countries. The WILPF's mission to Haiti, for example, was conducted by Emily Balch with a knowledgeable staff. Their investigation resulted in the study *Occu-*

pied Haiti (1927), which recommended to President Hoover that the United States Marines' occupation, since 1915, be ended.[26] (Hoover's independent investigation reached the same conclusion, and the Marines left in 1934.) From the 1920s, WILPF instructors in various countries were effective in peace education in summer schools. Also, the WILPF worked with the League of Nations throughout the 1920s and acknowledged its achievements and weaknesses in WILPF publications circulated to the League of Nations and to governments.[27]

The U.S. WILPF, alone of American women's peace groups, would survive the vicissitudes of the 1930s and 1940s. All along, however, it endured disagreements from the petty and personal to the more serious and ideological centered on how to implement the agreed ends. Behind each achievement there were struggles to create the expected consensus. Although absolute pacifists often disapproved of Detzer's tactics, a major accomplishment, all agreed, was her successful lobbying on Capitol Hill for an investigation of munitions makers. She and the WILPF took satisfaction in the famous Nye Commission enquiry in 1934 that publicized the activities of munitions makers in World War I, alerting the public to the danger of arms build-up. But in the second half of the 1930s, it became impossible for the leadership to attain the consensus desired by all.[28]

In retrospect, 1932, the year of the Geneva Disarmament Conference, marked the end of an early period of hopefulness for peace reformers. The ineffectiveness of the conference, with its minimal presence of women delegates, presaged the confusion and disagreement of nations and peoples soon faced with new threats to the world's peace. One aggressive act followed another in different parts of the world: Bolivia's and Paraguay's assaults on each other (1928 and 1932), Japan's invasion of Manchuria (1931), Mussolini's attack on Ethiopia (1935), and the Spanish Civil War (1936–1939) followed by Japan's attack on China's northern provinces in 1937. Finally, Hitler's takeover of western Europe, beginning with his dictatorship in Germany in 1933, led to German reoccupation of the Rhineland (1935) and Hitler's drive through Europe. After his Anschluss (union) with Austria (March 1938), his promises at Munich (September 1938) proved meaningless, for then followed

Germany's invasion of Czechoslovakia and Poland in 1939. Great Britain and France declared war on Germany, and Hitler continued his attacks in Denmark, Norway, Holland, Belgium, France, and England.[29]

Initially, Americans observed reluctantly this course of undeclared acts of war by Japan, Italy, and Germany that contributed to the breakdown of international agreements. Neither the United States government nor other western nations wanted to respond forcefully. By the same token, American leaders of peace groups did not agree on strategies for maintaining peace. How could one ignore the evils let loose in the world and at the same time live up to the ideals of peace, justice, and freedom? Not only pacifists, but other Americans, opposed United States participation in another world war when that war appeared more and more a likely possibility.

For Americans, the central question became how to preserve United States neutrality and keep out of the pending European war. National policy in neutrality legislation from 1935 to 1939 revolved around the issue of mandatory versus discretionary neutrality. Ironically, the peace groups, earlier in favor of discriminatory arms embargoes to prevent aggression, now reversed their view to insist on a neutrality that made no distinction between belligerents and victims. The leadership in the U.S. WILPF split with Dorothy Detzer and Hannah Hull, who upheld mandatory neutrality, and Emily Balch and Mildred Olmsted, who advocated discretionary neutrality.[30]

The WILPF leadership had argued about this issue from the time of Japan's invasion of Manchuria and Hitler's election to the Reichstag, both in the early 1930s. Hannah Hull, president of the WILPF in 1937–1938 and representative of the majority of members, declared that the organization had not become isolationist but still believed in cooperation:

The rock on which we stumble is that of naming the aggressor nation and applying to it coercive measures, especially in the conviction that economic sanctions would necessarily lead to military sanctions.

She blamed the emergence of Hitler and Nazism on Germany's economic problems derived from the reparations clauses in the Versailles Treaty.[31]

Both sides, Hull/Detzer and Balch/Olmsted, offered arguments and proposals for consideration by the membership of the U.S. WILPF. Balch asserted that the position of neutrality "is as impractical as it is amoral, that it is none of our business what other countries do so long as they do not tread on our toes." By contrast Detzer stated,

The real way the United States could help keep war out of the world would be by striving to organize a world government—not by taking sides in the old imperialistic struggle for the control of Europe—by trade agreements with other nations, and by helping in every constructive way possible to deal with the basic factors making for world chaos.

Despite concerted efforts of each side to persuade the other, the polling of the American WILPF membership in 1939 showed that the members voting could not reach a consensus; the majority continued to favor mandatory neutrality. There was no sense of triumph on the part of Detzer and Hull; rather they as well as Balch and Olmsted agonized with awareness that neither side had convinced the other.[32]

Not only did the members of the U.S. WILPF disagree among themselves, but they were unable to reconcile sharp differences with the WILPF leaders of the European sections. As early as 1933, on the continent heads of French, Belgian, Swiss, and German sections unequivocally opposed neutrality. As the French leader Gabrielle Duchene wrote in 1937, neutrality was "a mirage."[33]

These Europeans took note of the dangers in fascism and Nazism for women as well as Marxists, pacifists, and Jews. And the German WILPF leaders like Lida G. Heymann and Gertrud Baer, who had read *Mein Kampf,* had no illusions about the goals of Hitlerism. As historian Linda Fabrizio has noted, such continental activists found themselves increasingly distanced not only from the U.S. WILPF but from the English and Scandinavian sections. While all the European sections recognized the profound menace to humanity in fascism and Nazism for the whole world, they disagreed on the means that they would employ to attack and defeat these evils. Some WILPF continentalists in desperation were ready to cooperate with other groups, including those on the Left like communists, of whom they disapproved. A few were willing to go beyond their moral suasion, that is even to countenance violent tactics to defeat fascism. Such tactics were unacceptable under any circumstances to Quakers like Edith Pye of the English WILPF, among others. As in the growing divisions among the American WILPF leaders, so the Europeans' showed marked strains. In part, the English and Scandinavians were motivated by self-protection, like their governments' leaders, until appeasement of Hitler failed after Munich. Yet, despite the ambivalences affecting their responses, the non–continentalists gave what support they could to their sisters in the countries affected as war spread all over western Europe.[34]

By the same token, in the United States, while other women's peace groups faltered in 1939 and 1940, the U.S. WILPF section, chapters, and leaders, and those members who did not resign managed to admit basic disagreements and yet respect each other even though they could no longer reach their intended and valued consensus. Not only in the WILPF but in the larger American society it became difficult to maintain the illusion of neutrality even though most citizens supported nonintervention in what was still a European war. In fact, wartime preparedness in the United States gradually produced a significant change in public opinion. Increasingly by 1940, the majority of Americans favored all kinds of aid to Britain short of war.[35]

Within the WILPF, American leaders stayed divided until Japan attacked the United States at Pearl Harbor on 7 December 1941. Earlier that year, the *Washington Merry Go Round* reported that Emily Balch had resigned from WILPF because she differed with its public stand for mandatory neutrality. The latter fact was true, but Balch had no intention of resigning. To Drew Pearson, Miss Balch explained what was essentially the Quaker method, though not so labeled:

As regards a show down within the organization we have fortunately a continuous series of them in the shape of votes on controversial issues. In general those who are voted down continue with the organization to try to perform the functions of "his Majesty's Opposition."[36]

For Balch and other deeply conflicted Quakers, World War II posed the most painful dilemma over the testimony of freedom for all races against the potential absolutism of the peace testimony. To herself and good friends, Balch acknowledged her personal ambivalence. In true Quaker fashion she knew that hers was a conflict over two different testimonies. Similarly, D. Elton Trueblood, then professor of the philosophy of religion at Stanford, admitted the "moral predicament" in staying with the peace testimony despite the costs to European society from the spread of Nazism. Still Trueblood and other Quakers did not cease to respect individuals' choices in conflicts over testimonies honestly arrived at.[37]

Privately, Emily Balch, in a lengthy letter to Dr. Alice Hamilton, reviewed her thinking and distinguished it from the different view of absolute pacifists. For her part Balch stated,

it is *not* enough to sweep before your own door, not to cultivate your own garden, nor to put out the fire when your own house is burning and "disinterest yourself", [*sic*] as the diplomats say, when the frame house next door is in flames and the children calling from its nursery windows to be taken out.[38]

She recalled that at its international conference at Vienna in 1921 the WILPF had voted not to require of all members a pledge of war resistance. But Balch, having revealed her own conviction, stated that there are "100% absolutist religious pacifists—of whom I have never been one. I stop being non-resistant when it is a question of offering my neighbor's cheek for the blow." Nonetheless, Balch conveyed her respect for the absolutists: "I thank God for the Conscientious Objectors. . . . They fulfill a function which [Elton] Trueblood in his excellent article in the December *Atlantic* accepts as the sole justification of pacifism—that of 'bearing witness.' "[39]

In contrast to Balch's antiwar stand in World War I, what now became critical to her in making a decision about World War II was Hitler and his supporters who "make a religion of force." Emily Balch knew she was choosing among evils but felt it her "duty to *stay in the world* and try to make it better in such ways as are practically open to one." Thus, she sided with the European WILPF leaders.[40]

Balch did not arrive at her decision without struggle. She knew that absolute pacifists in the U.S. section would condemn her decision. Indeed one, author Anna Graves, wrote with the strongest disapproval to her on 5 April 1942: "Dear Emily, Oh! If you would only repudiate your repudiation!"

Can't you see that Peace Societies can never have any effect when Governments *see* that when war comes they always crumble?—that their leaders are sure not to keep their faith when trial comes? What incentive is there for joining any cause when one sees that one cannot count on the loyalty even of the leaders to their own cause? You often thought that Alice Paul was not all she should be, but at any rate her own cause can count on her loyalty to it—her *absolute* loyalty.[41]

Anna Graves's point rested on the logic of absolute pacifism. Thereafter, the letter deteriorated into personal resentment against the presumed influence of one member of the executive committee, Gertrud Baer, a founding member of the German section of the WILPF in 1915. This German–Jewish feminist, who managed to escape from Germany (with the help of Dorothy Detzer and others), was representative of the European leaders in the WILPF who welcomed American participation in World War II. Baer herself was a survivor who would build up WILPF work in the United Nations in the 1950s, among her numerous other commitments.[42]

It is simplistic to assume that absolute pacifists had no conflicts. Undoubtedly some, both Quakers and others, did not question their peace testimony, but surely some did. I have found evidence of a literature on this in public testimonies of Quaker men, but not of Quaker women. Women appear to have kept their conflicts more private; even Emily Balch's was written in a private letter. I hope that further exploration of the papers of women pacifists will produce evidence about their personal dilemmas.[43]

The conflicts of some women became manifest in their actions. Gertrude Bussey, for example, resigned the presidency of the U.S. WILPF because she felt a forthright pacifist should be the president. Once the United States entered the war, individuals in the American WILPF supported conscientious objectors and other humanitarian projects. Also, they dealt with new political issues confronting women.

Not many Americans in general, nor pacifists and feminists in particular, thought that equality of the sexes should be applied to conscription in the armed services. Some leaders in the National

Woman's Party as well as the Women's Bureau of the federal government (usually not on the same side on women's issues), along with Quakers, spoke forcefully against women's conscription. Jessie Hughan of the War Resisters League appealed to Dorothy Detzer to lobby for the protection of women as well as male conscientious objectors. Many U.S. WILPF members joined the Women's Committee to Oppose Conscription, directed by Mildred Olmsted. Even though relatively few Americans, men or women, were ready to support legislation requiring women to enter the armed services despite the example in England, there was considerable controversy about the issue in 1942. Interestingly, four out of five readers of the *Independent Woman,* then published by the General Federation of Business and Professional Women's Clubs, did favor compulsory registration of American women for war services. Eleanor Roosevelt, unlike Franklin Roosevelt, favored voluntary registration of women between the ages of eighteen and sixty-five. Nevertheless, the plan to require women to enter the armed services never gained sufficient support and was not acted upon.[44]

Still, the war soon increased opportunities for women to enter the labor force as men left for the armed forces. For women pacifists, such opportunities created a new dilemma. As one who experienced it wrote,

as the war effort began to evolve . . . [it] needed women as the men were drafted, and new gains were to be made in opportunities for women in war industries and in the armed services. Women who were feminists as well as pacifists had the dilemma of working for expanded opportunities for women, or maintaining their absolute pacifism and not being involved in the war effort.[45]

The war made possible opportunities for women at every level of employment. Alice Paul, though still removed from active pacifism and enraged that her work for women's equality should be interrupted again, nonetheless supported the women doctors seeking to serve in the armed forces on an equal basis with men in their profession. Thus once again, pacifism and feminism in wartime generated conflicts over priorities for women.[46]

Over the course of the twentieth century, women reformers have worked cumulatively to advance the ideals of pacifism and feminism and at the same time aimed to sustain patriotism in a world torn by international crises. Inevitably, the interconnections between pacifism and a politically framed feminism devoted to national issues evoked dilemmas taking different forms at particular times. From the perspective of the 1980s, pacifism appears to be a more widely accepted principle than earlier in the century. The potential for nuclear destruction of the whole world brings a new urgency to peace. And yet currently Quaker, as well as non-Quaker, women in America and England find in feminism a source of new awakenings and new dilemmas. In Quaker idiom, it is not now the peace testimony that precipitates conflict but the testimony for equality of women within the meeting and the world. As we have seen, earlier generations of Quaker activists, with the notable exception of Alice Paul, placed the cause of peace ahead of women's equality.

Those who struggle in the 1980s with confrontations between religious faith and feminism may learn from the history recounted here about the complexity in women's choices in working for peace and freedom in times of public conflict. It is understandable in view of the nature of the mounting international problems over the first half of the twentieth century that pacifists (like other Americans) disagreed on how to resolve the crises that erupted into worldwide war. Quakers found that abiding by one testimony meant cutting off or lessening commitment to another. So pacifism and feminism or pacifism and democracy or pacifism and freedom for all races could not be sustained in particular situations. Pacifists had to make hard choices as the nature of their conflicts changed with the changing issues. Significantly, Quaker women and those who worked with them learned that even though their disagreements seemed unavoidable, they could still apply the method of consensus to ease the strains of conflict. The Quaker approach stands as a model for reformers in which respect for individual choices of conscience and understanding of differing convictions can bring a measure of strength and harmony to a troubled group. With this awareness, the Women's International League for Peace and Freedom, dominated by its Quaker leadership, survived World War II while other peace organizations disappeared.[47]

A new generation of scholars has embarked on comparative

studies of the role of women in European and North American peace groups; their work is much needed. Historians should also learn more about the influence of Quaker women in religious meetings and other Quaker organizations. I am still concerned with understanding the inner Quaker motive and thought that validates the method of consensus. I urge scholars to explore further this process by which Quaker women become their own witnesses for change.[48]

NOTES

In preparing this essay, I benefited from the generosity of the following, whom I thank: Harriet Hyman Alonso, Margaret Bacon, Elisabeth Potts Brown, Wendy E. Chmielewski, Margaret Dollar, Frances Early, Linda Fabrizio, Amelia Fry, Karen Morgan, Mildred Scott Olmsted, Anne Marie Pois, Jean Soderlund, George St. John, and Elizabeth Watson.

1. According to *Webster's New International Dictionary* (1952), "pacifism" is defined as "opposition to war or to the use of military force for any purpose; esp., an attitude of mind opposing all war, emphasizing the defects of military training and the cost of war, and advocating settlement of international disputes entirely by arbitration; also, the system of beliefs of opinions opposing war or the use of military force"; *The Shorter Oxford English Dictionary on Historical Principles* defines "pacifism" as "the doctrine of belief that it is desirable and possible to settle international disputes by peaceful means."

2. Howard H. Brinton, *The Peace Testimony of the Society of Friends* (Philadelphia: American Friends Service Committee, 1958); Peter Brock, *Pioneers of the Peaceable Kingdom* (Princeton: Princeton University Press, 1968). For excellent historical background, see Howard H. Brinton, *Friends for 300 Years* (New York: Harper, 1952).

3. In conversation, Carol Stoneburner, director of faculty development and coordinator of women's studies at Guilford College, and director of the Symposium on American Quaker Women as Shapers of Human Space, Guilford College, 1979, confirmed this point about the peace testimony for me. See Lawrence Scott on the origin of the peace witness in *Faith and Practice* (Worcester, Mass.: New England Yearly Meeting of Friends, 1985) 183; Scott distinguishes it from the witness against war (personal correspondence to Barbara Solomon from George St. John). See also Merle Curti, *Peace or War: The American Struggle, 1636–1936* (New York: W.W. Norton, 1936).

4. On the shift of woman's rights leaders to peace work, see Margaret Hope Bacon, *Mothers of Feminism* (San Francisco: Harper & Row, 1986). See also C. Roland Marchand, *The American Peace Movement and Social Reform, 1898–1918* (Princeton: Princeton University Press, 1972), 15–16, 105–109. Unitarian minister Charles Dole is an example of an active pacifist during the Spanish-American War. He greatly influenced the young Emily Balch, a member of his congregation. See Barbara Miller Solomon, *Ancestors and Immigrants: A Changing New England Tradition* (Cambridge: Harvard University Press, 1956), chap. 9.

5. On Fannie Fern Andrews and Lucia Ames Mead, see biographical essays in Edward T. and Janet Wilson James, eds., *Notable American Women, 1607–1950: A Biographical Dictionary*, vols. 1 and 2, respectively (Cambridge: Harvard University Press, 1971). On Hannah Clothier Hull, see Carol Stoneburner's "Timeline" in the Appendix

of Carol and John Stoneburner, eds., *The Influence of Quaker Women on American History: Biographical Studies* (Lewiston, N.Y.: Mellen, 1986); and Margaret Bacon, "The Widening Path: Women in the Philadelphia Yearly Meeting Move Toward Equality, 1681–1929," in John M. Moore, ed., *Friends in the Delaware Valley, Philadelphia Yearly Meeting, 1681–1981* (Haverford, Pa.: Friends Historical Association, 1981).

6. Charles Chatfield, "World War I and the Liberal Pacifist in the United States," *American Historical Review* 75 (December 1970): 1920–1937; Jane Addams, Emily Greene Balch, and Alice Hamilton, *Women at The Hague: The International Congress of Women and its Results* (1915; rpt. New York: Garland Publishing, 1972).

7. Barbara Miller Solomon, "Emily Greene Balch and the Tradition of Peace: New England Brahmin and Convinced Quaker," in Stoneburner and Stoneburner, *The Influence of Quaker Women*. See also Frances H. Early, "The Historic Roots of the Women's Peace Movement in North America," *Canadian Woman Studies* 7 (Winter 1986): 43–48; and Frances H. Early to Barbara Miller Solomon, 26 February 1987. Frances Witherspoon, Tracy Mygatt, and Jessie Hughan, who were suffragists and by 1915 pacifists as well, experienced no dilemmas, for they were single-minded in their commitment to peace. Witherspoon was born a Catholic and became an Episcopalian because Mygatt was (the two were a "couple"). Hughan was Unitarian.

8. Emily Greene Balch to Ellen Pendleton, 30 March 1918, Balch Papers (on microfilm), Swarthmore College Peace Collection, Swarthmore College, Swarthmore, Pa. (hereafter cited as SCPC).

9. In 1921, Emily Balch would apply from Geneva for membership in the Society of Friends of London. Barbara Miller Solomon, "Emily Greene Balch and the Tradition of Peace." See also Barbara Miller Solomon, "Emily Greene Balch," in Barbara Sicherman and Carol Hurd Green, eds., *Notable American Women*, vol. 4 (Cambridge: Harvard University Press, 1980).

10. On Catt's effort to be even-handed in working for the war and for suffrage, see Eleanor Flexner, *Century of Struggle: The Woman's Rights Movement in the United States* (Cambridge: Harvard University Press, 1959; rpt. New York: Atheneum, 1970), 289; and J. Stanley Lemons, *The Woman Citizen: Social Feminism in the 1920s* (Urbana: University of Illinois Press, 1973), 6. On Blatch's elation with the experience of war, see Lemons, 15.

11. Alice Paul, "Conversations With Alice Paul: Woman Suffrage and the Equal Rights Amendment, An Interview Conducted by Amelia Fry in 1972" (Berkeley: The Bancroft Library, University of California, 1976), 175ff. As in World War I, Alice Paul's pacifist faith was subsumed in feminism during World War II. Indeed, when forced to come home from Switzerland in April 1941, Paul declared publicly, "This war is a man-made war. We have got our world organization well underway. . . . What we plan to do is to have something to say when peace is discussed. Women must never again be excluded from the affairs of the world." Amelia Fry to Barbara Miller Solomon, 8 March 1987; see *World Telegram*, 3 April 1941, for quote. For more details, see Amelia R. Fry, "Alice Paul," in Stoneburner and Stoneburner, *The Influence of Quaker Women*.

12. At the National Woman's Party's 1921 Convention, many wanted the NWP's future to focus on world disarmament. After "heated debate," Alice Paul's close supporters made sure that the Resolution on World Disarmament was voted down despite strong interest in it. Soon after the NWP Convention, some leaders helped in the forming of a Women's Committee for World Disarmament to mobilize other groups. See Dorothy M. Brown, *Setting A Course: American Women in the 1920s* (Boston: Twayne

Publishers, 1987), 64; and Nancy F. Cott, *The Grounding of Modern Feminism* (New Haven: Yale University Press, 1987), 70–71, 244–245.

13. Religiously affiliated organizations ranged from the Federation of Women's Boards of Foreign Missions of North America, the National Board of the Young Women's Christian Associations, and the National Council of Jewish Women to the National Federation of Temple Sisterhoods, the Service Star Legion, and the Women's Missionary Union of Friends in America. Among the groups that focused on various reforms and/or professional interests were the National League of Women Voters, the National Women's Christian Temperance Union, the National Women's Trade Union League, the National Federation of Business and Professional Women's Clubs, the National Council of Nurses, and the American Association of University Women. Florence Brewer Boeckel, "Women in International Affairs," *Annals of the American Academy of Political and Social Science,* 143 (May 1929): 230–248.

14. Boeckel, "Women in International Affairs." According to Nancy Cott, the National Congress of Parents and Teachers Associations was one of the fastest-growing organizations, and it believed that public schools had a responsibility to educate children for peace. Cott, *The Grounding of Modern Feminism,* 87.

15. In a personal letter to me, Anne Marie Pois agrees with my assessment here. Anne Marie Pois to Barbara Miller Solomon, 3 July 1987.

16. Joan M. Jensen, "All Pink Sisters: The War Department and the Feminist Movement in the 1920s," in Lois Scharf and Joan M. Jensen, eds., *Decades of Discontent: The Women's Movement, 1920–1940* (Westport, Conn.: Greenwood Press, 1983). The WPU was founded in Niagara Falls in 1921 by a Toronto businesswoman; it campaigned for an amendment to the U. S. Constitution to make war unlawful. See also Early, "Historic Roots," 46.

17. Dorothy Detzer Denny to Barbara Miller Solomon, 27 January 1979. A copy of this letter is in Dorothy Detzer Denny's Papers, SCPC.

18. Jensen, "All Pink Sisters," 210–212 (for quote, see 212). See also Cott, *The Grounding of Modern Feminism,* 242, 249–250, 259; and Gertrude Bussey and Margaret Tims, *Pioneers for Peace: Women's International League for Peace and Freedom, 1915–1965* (London: WILPF British Section, 1980), 42–156, passim.

19. Anne Marie Pois points out to me that "the Pennsylvania branch of the WILPF was the largest and most wealthy branch," and undoubtedly "largely Quaker." Anne Marie Pois to Barbara Miller Solomon, 3 July 1987. For use of the term *Quaker-related,* see Bacon, *Mothers of Feminism,* 20. On Emily Balch, see Mercedes Randall, *Improper Bostonian: Emily Greene Balch* (New York: Twayne, 1964), and Barbara Miller Solomon, "Emily Greene Balch." On Mildred Scott Olmsted, see Jacqueline Van Voris, *College: A Smith Mosaic* (Northampton: Smith College, 1975), 29–31. On Dorothy Detzer, see her *Appointment on the Hill* (New York: Henry Holt, 1940). Interestingly, Quakers did not become members of the Women's Peace Union. According to Harriet Alonso, "The women [in the WPU] were a combination of Dutch Reformists, Episcopalians, Jews, socialists and athiests. . . . They were all non-resistors and admired Ghandi, William Lloyd Garrison, etc." Harriet Alonso to Barbara Miller Solomon, 31 March 1987.

20. Over time Emily Balch held all the major offices in the WILPF; Hannah Clothier Hull was president from 1924 to 1939; Mildred Scott Olmsted served as executive secretary from 1935 to 1949; and Lucy Biddle Lewis attended the original conference at The Hague. Francis Early, "An Interview with Mildred Scott Olmsted: Foremother of the Women's International League for Peace and Freedom," *Atlantis* 12 (Fall 1986), 142–150; and Stoneburner, "Timeline."

21. Lemons, *The Woman Citizen,* 210, 214–216; and Jensen, "All Pink Sisters," 216–217.

22. Early, "An Interview with Mildred Scott Olmsted," 145; and Harriet Hyman Alonso, "Putting Pacifism into Practice: Women Peace Activists and the Geneva Disarmament Conference of 1932" (Paper presented at the Seventh Berkshire Conference on the History of Women, Wellesley College, 21 June 1987). Furthermore, over the years male and female paid executive secretaries who were lobbyists frequently worked together, as Dorothy Detzer shows in her autobiography, *Appointment on the Hill.*

23. Some, dissatisfied with the churches in which they had been raised, became Quakers. See, for example, Elizabeth Watson to George St. John, Jr., 21 January 1987 (personal collection of Barbara Solomon).

24. Bussey and Tims, *Pioneers for Peace,* 124. Mildred Scott Olmsted explained to me in my presentation on 6 April 1987 at the Haverford College symposium "Witnesses for Change: Quaker Women, 1650–1987," that leaders of the European sections rejected the proposal and stated they would leave the organization if men were admitted. The Europeans said that in their countries they could not work with men in the organization. On the other reason for dropping the proposal to admit men (i.e., to preserve the organization that effectively promoted women's "different" values), see also the explanation in Early's interview with Olmsted, esp. 146–147.

25. Jensen, "All Pink Sisters," 199–222; Carrie Foster-Hayes, "The Women and the Warriors: Dorothy Detzer and the WILPF" (unpublished Ph.D. diss., University of Denver, 1984), 641; Anne Marie Pois, "The Crisis Years, 1935–39: The American Women of the Women's International League for Peace and Freedom Face the Dilemma of Fascism, Aggression and Neutrality" (Paper delivered to the Seventh Berkshire Conference on the History of Women, Wellesley College, 20 June 1987); WILPF, U.S. Section Records, Series A,2 Box 1, Annual Report for year ending April 1921; WILPF, U.S. Section Records, Series A,2 Box 2, Annual Statistical Report from the National Office to the 1930 Annual Meeting, May 15, 1930; and WILPF, U.S. Section Records, Series A,2 Box 9, Report of the National Organization Secretary to the Annual Meeting, April 27–30, 1940, all at SCPC.

26. Emily Greene Balch, ed., *Occupied Haiti* (New York: The Writer's Publishing Company, 1927).

27. At present, membership figures for the European sections are scant and in some cases appear to be nonexistent. According to Anne Marie Pois's assessment, the number of European members probably ranged between thirty and fifty thousand in the interwar period. Anne Marie Pois to Barbara Miller Solomon, 8 December 1987. According to the Swarthmore College Peace Collection, the Danish section seems to have reported most frequently: in 1929, 13,000 members; 1934, 20,000 members; and 1937, 25,000 members. For Great Britain the only figures were: 1921, 3635 members and 1924, 3500 members. See "Report of the 6th Congress of the WILPF," 135; "Minutes of Proceedings of the 8th Congress of the WILPF," 39; "Report of the 9th Congress of the WILPF," 150; "Report of the 3rd Congress of the WILPF," 225; and "Report of the 4th Congress of the WILPF," 13, all at SCPC.

28. Foster-Hayes, "The Women and the Warriors."

29. Alonso, "Putting Pacifism into Practice."

30. See Robert A. Divine, *The Illusion of Neutrality* (Chicago: University of Chicago Press, 1962); and Pois, "The Crisis Years."

31. Hannah Clothier Hull, National President, "Annual Report," U.S. WILPF, 1937–1938, Series A,2 Box 5, SCPC.

32. Emily Greene Balch, "A Foreign Policy For the W.I.L.," appended to Branch Letter 70, 28 February 1939, U.S. WILPF, Series E4, Fldr. 1939, SCPC; and Dorothy Detzer, "The Pro-Neutrality Pattern" (unsigned by Dorothy Detzer), appended to Branch Letter 70, 28 February 1939, U.S. WILPF, Series E4, Fldr. 1939, SCPC. Detzer and Balch had changed their opinions on the issue of sanctions against Japan; these women were not static in their thinking. See Anne Marie Pois to Barbara Miller Solomon, 28 September 1987. Nearly one thousand members voted with 75 percent supporting mandatory neutrality. The leaders interpreted these figures as representing the sentiment of the majority although not all members voted. See Pois, "The Crisis Years," endnote 31.

33. Neutrality as "a mirage," quoted in Pois, "The Crisis Years" (Gabrielle Duchene to the U.S. Section of the WILPF, 14 April 1937, U.S. WILPF, Series C1, Box 25, Fldr., International, 1937, SCPC). On the European climate of opinion, see Linda Fabrizio, "The Challenge Accepted: The European Women of WILPF Against Fascism" (Paper presented at the Seventh Berkshire Conference on the History of Women, Wellesley College, 20 June 1987).

34. Fabrizio, "The Challenge Accepted"; in addition, see Bussey and Tims, *Pioneers for Peace,* especially 156–157, the "official history" which emphasizes the support given by the English and Scandinavian WILPF to the continentalist sections during the war.

35. See "Public Opinion Poll About Intervention, 1939–1941" by Professor Hadley Cantril and the Public Opinion Research Project of Princeton University, reproduced in T. Harry Williams, Richard N. Current, and Frank Freidel, eds., *A History of the United States,* vol. 2, (New York: Alfred A. Knopf, 1959), 539.

36. Emily Greene Balch to Drew Pearson, 18 February 1941, WILPF Papers—U.S. Section, Correspondence, DG 43, Series C, Box 37, SCPC. Pois believes that Balch was going to resign from the American section but not from the International WILPF. A letter from Gertrude C. Bussey to Mr. Robert Allen affirms Balch's letter on the way policy was formulated in WILPF: "As a democratic organization we have always expected differences of opinion among our members. The frank discussion of such differences is an essential part of our program and contributes to the real strength of the League. To a person of a totalitarian type of mind, such discussion might have indicated a "cracking in our pacifist position" but to those of us who are familiar with the traditions of our League it indicated only an honest effort to face squarely the difficulties that confront all of us who wish to advance the cause of peace and freedom in the present world. All of this is stated in the first resolution which was unanimously adopted, as furnishing the framework of all the other decisions reached." Gertrude C. Bussey to Robert Allen, 27 January 1941, WILPF Papers—U.S. Section, Correspondence, DG 43, Series C, Box 37, SCPC.

37. D. Elton Trueblood, "The Quaker Way," *Atlantic Monthly* 166 (December 1940): 741.

38. Emily Greene Balch to Alice Hamilton, 20 February 1941, in the WILPF Papers—U.S. Section, Records, DG 43, Series C, Box 37, SCPC. Alice Hamilton concurred with her old friend Emily Balch; for Hamilton's attitudes toward World War II, see Barbara Sicherman, *Alice Hamilton: A Life in Letters* (Cambridge: Harvard University Press, 1984), 368.

39. Emily Greene Balch to Alice Hamilton, 20 February 1941.

40. Ibid.

41. Anna Graves to Emily Balch, 5 April 1942, in the Balch Papers, SCPC. Anna Graves ends her letter by blaming Americans and the Allies for not undermining Hitler-

ism by "giving Germany a chance to believe that she will have an equal share of what the earth affords."

42. See Detzer, *Appointment on the Hill;* Foster-Hayes, "The Women and the Warriors"; and biographical profile of Gertrud Baer in WILPF Papers—International, DG 43, Series A, Box 1a, SCPC.

43. Frances Early, who is writing on Frances Witherspoon and Tracy Mygatt (who were not Quakers), informs me that they never doubted their absolute pacifism. Frances H. Early to Barbara Miller Solomon, 26 February 1987. In addition to Trueblood, "The Quaker Way," see, for example, Brinton, *The Peace Testimony.* Also relevant as a model is the English 1986 Swarthmore Lecture written by an English Quaker women's group: Quaker Women's Group, *Bringing the Invisible Into the Light: Some Quaker Feminists Speak of Their Experience* (London: Quaker Home Service, 1986). The lecture emphasizes contemporary conflicts of Quakerism and feminism, not pacifism. Hannah Clothier Hull and her husband, both Quaker-born and educated at Swarthmore College, lived their lives as witnesses for peace. And both suffered from public attacks for their commitments. Frederick B. Tolles, "Partners for Peace: William I. Hull and Hannah Clothier Hull," *Swarthmore Alumni Issue,* 3 (December 1958): 44–45. Jean Soderlund, curator of the Swarthmore College Peace Collection, could not find a statement concerning personal dilemmas in the papers of Hannah Clothier Hull.

44. The Women's Bureau was opposed to the Equal Rights Amendment that the National Woman's Party proselytized. On Jessie Hughan, see Jessie Wallace Hughan to Dorothy Detzer, 25 September 1942, and Dorothy Detzer to Jessie Wallace Hughan, 12 October 1942, WILPF Papers—U.S. Section, DG 43, Series C, Box 39, SCPC. On the issue of registering women for war service, see "On Registering Women," *Independent Woman* 26: 5, (1919): 145–146; and Maurine Beasley, ed., *The White House Press Conferences of Eleanor Roosevelt* (New York and London: Garland Publishing, 1983). By contrast, journalist and academic Max Lerner, who claimed he was for equality of education, favored compulsory drafting of women if necessary; see Caroline Lerow Babcok and Olive E. Hurlbert Papers, Folder A-117, National Woman's Party, 1943, Schlesinger Library, Radcliffe College.

45. Elizabeth Watson to George St. John, Jr., 21 January 1987. A copy of this letter was supplied by George St. John, Jr.

46. Amelia R. Fry to Barbara Miller Solomon, 8 March 1987.

47. Quaker Women's Group, *Bringing the Invisible Into the Light.*

48. In this context, Margaret Bacon, "A Widening Path," offers enlightenment.

DOCUMENTS

In the preceding essay, we have observed a spectrum of attitudes among individuals and groups of American women reacting to the breakdown of international agreements and illegal military aggressions on every continent. As Europe hovered on the verge of war, the U. S. Congress passed neutrality laws from 1935 to 1938 with the intent of keeping America out of war. The legislation deliberately made no distinction between aggressors and victims. The European sections of the Women's International League for Peace and Freedom (WILPF) were appalled; the United States section of the WILPF held intense discussions and debate about the merit of these laws. The majority, represented by the arguments of Hannah Clothier Hull and Dorothy Detzer, favored the existing mandatory neutrality, and the minority, represented by Emily Greene Balch and Mildred Scott Olmsted, supported discriminatory neutrality that would permit the United States to aid the victims and penalize the aggressors. Hannah Clothier Hull, in her presidential report of 1937–1938, which is excerpted here, expressed the constructive goals of the entire membership along with justifications for the position of mandatory neutrality.

In the worsening crisis, with Europe actually at war from 1939, Emily Greene Balch, in a private letter in the Emily Greene Balch Papers, Swarthmore College Peace Collection, shared her innermost conflict about the role of the United States. Balch, who had publicly opposed American entrance into World War I, now found herself unable to stay with the stand of absolute pacifism because of the presence of Hitler's plan to liquidate all but his own "master race."

Both documents reprinted here reveal the common concerns of the WILPF leaders and the different lines they drew for the price of peace. Balch's letter conveys the personal religious passions that enabled her to make her choice in a profound dilemma.

Annual Report

Hannah Clothier Hull, National President.

Women's International League for Peace and Freedom
1937–1938

The last year has been a testing time for all of us both individually and collectively. We have had to think through our policies more searchingly than ever before and the conclusions of one individual are not those of another, nor has the experience of one Branch been necessarily that of another as we have endeavored to apply our common principles.

IT HAPPENS at the moment that the policies of the United States Section do not co-incide with the actions and resolutions of the International Executive Committee.

Our difficulties have been augmented by the fact that our U.S. neutrality legislation was misnamed. Our European sisters had, therefore, thought of it in terms of the pre-war idea of neutrality—the neutrality of Switzerland, Belgium, and Luxembourg and also in the sense of isolation, as have many of our own American citizens so considered it.

We of the United States Section who have stood for the Neutrality legislation repudiate completely the charge that our so called neutrality today spells isolation from, or irresponsibility toward, the rest of the world. The W.I.L. is far from an isolationist organization. It is first of all cooperative. The rock on which we stumble is that of naming the aggressor nation and applying to it coercive measures, especially in the conviction that economic sanctions would necessarily lead to military sanctions. It is not a new experience to have difference of opinion among us. In this connection I venture to quote to you some sentences from the preamble and the resolutions adopted by our founders at the Hague in 1915.

"However we may differ as to means we declare ourselves united in the great ideals of civilization and progress impelled by profoundly humane forces and bound together by the beliefs that women must share in the common responsibility of government and that international relations must be determined not by force but by friendship and justice, we pledge ourselves to promote mutual understanding and good-will between the nations and to work for the reconciliation of the peoples."

THE TASK before *us* today as a group is still to consider what ways we can make our special and peculiar contribution toward bringing about the things for which we have stood from the beginning. Are they not sufficiently numerous and important that we maintain our own separate organization? Yes, I believe they are and our loyalty to them must not swerve. We have a responsibility to act as we think best on measures as they arise but also to keep alive in the world our original points of view and all the traditions of the W.I.L. from its inception, not as traditions or because they are traditions, even though they are our own, but because they are live issues today. We see now, and Dorothy Detzer brought out the fact in *Fellowship,* that the visions heralded by Miss Addams and our founders at the 1915 Congress have not yet been fulfilled and until they are we should indeed be recreant to our trust were we to depart from the determination made there. We of today must not minimize our task as they did not at the Hague in 1915.

Our task still is two-fold (1) to help remove the causes of war and (2) to persuade governments to use the machinery of Peace.

The economist tells us that the causes of war are *economic*.

Governments say that they are *political*.

Psychologists say that they are entirely *psychological,* and we of the W.I.L. know that they are a combination of all three.

Our program is constructive and should and does include measures crying to be carried out:

1. abolition of imperialism, first in our own country,
2. of the armament system which nurtures imperialism,
3. of tariff barriers and
4. of race discrimination including the oriental exclusion act.

Support of:

1. the holding of genuine international peace conferences,
2. just and humane measures for the care of political exiles and stateless persons,
3. the constant advocacy of the use of Peace machinery in definite terms of the United States entering the World Court.
4. strict adherence to Treaties, the Kellogg Pact in particular,
5. the Van Zeeland[1] report and of other plans for the promotion of international trade which are before the world for consideration.

THE PEACE sentiment over our country is so great that those who believe in armed force and military preparedness are worried and have been busily organizing propaganda to counteract it. May we "beat them to it," so to speak, and get in our peace education first.

ALL OF US believe in the same ultimate end. While we strive toward it, may we not make it impossible by the means we use to achieve it, but above all, keep our eye on the *ultimate* goal,—a warless world,—not a world without differences, but a world with constructive and peaceful means of settling differences as they arise. The method of force has been proved to be a fallacious theory. On the other hand, the success of peaceful machinery when given a chance, has been proved many times.

May we of the W.I.L. make our contribution as best we can toward the practical as well as the ethical means of avoiding war, and may we Thank God if we "find ourselves matched" to this difficult hour in which to do it.

The W.I.L.P.F. had a clear vision in 1915. We have tried for 23 years to follow it in a changing world. It can not be that we shall lose sight of that vision in this tragic hour—the vision, namely, of a united international women's movement for Peace in every land among all peoples and thus to help create, in the words of Frauelein Heymann, "the solidarity of the whole world."

Emily Greene Balch's letter to Alice Hamilton

20 February 1941

Dear Alice Hamilton:

Thanks for your letter of February 17. The statement in the *Washington Merry Go Round* is absolutely incorrect.[2] I am *not* resigning and never said I should do so. I said something evidently that was misunderstood by one of our members who started this false report which, of course, I shall never catch up with. I note first to Drew Pearson as I had been told that he wrote the distinctly unpleasant paragraph with its fling at D.D. (who is an old friend of Drew Pearson's,) which hurt me.[3] I wrote him and he wrote a really friendly and nice letter and referred me to Mr. Allen.[4] After some days Mr. Allen wrote a retraction, grudging and not happily worded, I thought, taking back the statement that I had resigned. It is some satisfaction that this appeared in the Merry Go Round syndicated column, but I could wish it had been done more handsomely. How well a little magnanimity sits on one.

Thanks for sending me Bertrand Russell's article.[5] It is finely put, isn't it? And I think it is my position. I think Hutchins[6] was simply preposterous as B.R. so neatly exposes.

People say this country is confused, divided and chaotic, etc. I must say that it appears to me that the great mass are united to a surprising degree and with no more than quite wholesome divergences. I seem to see: wide agreement *on aid of all kinds to Britain short of war;* somewhat smaller body of opinion within this ready successively for a) policy that risks war, b) military intervention (much smaller). Then, on the other end: a) opposition due to fear of excessive executive power, b) pagan isolationism which, in my opinion, has no leg to stand on, either realist or moral, c) those who believe one should begin with making democracy (nearly) perfect in the U.S. and *then* concern ourselves with helping to clean up other peoples' messes. ("Charity begins at home" to often means "and ends there.")

It is *not* enough to sweep before your own door, nor to cultivate your own garden, nor to put out the fire when your own house is burning and "disinterest yourself," as the diplomats say, when the frame house next door is in flames and the children calling from its nursery windows to be taken out.

d) Then there are the 100% absolutist religious pacifists—of whom I have never been one.

I stop being non-resistant when it is a question of offering my neighbor's cheek for the blow. As a matter of fact I am not 100% non-resistant even in what concerns only myself.

At the same time I thank God for the Conscientious Objectors. There are not enough of them to prevent action and they are highly educational and their purity, if not true wisdom, is a definite contribution to present and future. They fulfill the function which Elwood Trueblood in his excellent article in the December *Atlantic* accepts as the sole justification of pacifism—that of "bearing witness." I am glad some have the vocation for this, though I have not. Of course if we could have had pacifism equally strong and articulate in Germany, etc. as well as on the side of freedom, it would all have been different. The trouble with the peace movement—there was such—was that it was aborted and rooted out where it was most needed. A *unilateral* pacifism is not what we were working for.

And here let me say that I do not see evidence that the W.I.L.P.F. as such (or J.A.[7] even) committed themselves to the 100% pacifist position. Where moral resistance a la Gandhi[8] is possible—well and good. But his *success* rests, I think, not only on the greater moral maturity of Indians in the matter of non-violence, but on the common moral bases of Indians and English which gave a *pou sto*[9] for the pressure on English opinion which was the measure of Gandhi's success.

I am far from admitting that it is not true as we Quakers believe, that "there is that of God in everyman." But I do not believe that there is *now* "that" in Hitler et al. that responds with magnanimity to the non-resistant virtues. I would not say they "understand nothing but force," but I would say that they make a religion of force which makes them impervious along those lines. At the same time they may be capable of more "sacrificial" self-giving than we are to what they believe is the cause of advance. Alas, this seems to mean to them "Woe to the weak." "Liquidate the 'other' "—(Jew Pole Negro). "Make straight the path for the powerful, able, noble master-race. This is the way of the Gods."

I believe this is devil's doctrine but not that the men who are hypnotized by it are necessarily devils.

To return to the W.I.L. We refused in Vienna to vote to require pledges of war resistance. We pledged ourselves at Zurich[10] to do everything we could for peace for which I believe now (as I did then) no sacrifice is too great.

The question is how is peace, or any chance of peace, to be secured. The answer that I could make before Hitler is not the sam [illegible] could make now in the face of entirely unforeseeable developments—incredible, even while one knows them to be true.

I am not at all sure Willkie is not right in believing that *as things are now* our best chance of peace as a nation (to say nothing of world peace) is to help to try to put down Hitlerism.

I am not very hopeful. I *am* afraid. I cannot feel that there is now any path that has a chance of leading forward that is not a bloody one and a long one.

My position is that peoples by their crimes and blunders can get themselves into a position where on the *plane of political action* there is only a choice of evils.

One can withdraw from this world and let it go on its own wicked way. If one feels it is a duty to *stay in the world* and try to make it better in such ways as are practically open to one, then one is in for all the intolerable consequences of the fighting method and its competition in the cruelist of "skin games" (referring to Galsworthy's wonderful play of that name). And perhaps hunger blockade is the most disastrous weapon of all.

This sounds horribly like Nieboer [sic][11] whom I loathe! To such bed-fellows one comes. And I don't think I hate his lingo more than the "sacrificial" talk. A mother gives all to her child but not as a sacrifice. To set out to sacrifice oneself or urge others to do so is psychologically and ethically bad, it seems to me. The point is not the cost but the achieving what you aim at. If you care enough, cost is not a problem, and to dwell on sacrifice as if it were fine in itself leads too easily to moral priggishness. It sets self in the center. Or so I see it.

Excuse this long and ill thought-out discussion. It represents the present state of my yeasty mind. And I am not happy in it, of course.

Affectionately yours,

[The following paragraphs appear to be a postscript to the letter.] To sum up, this is how it now seems to me.

England has got herself involved in war and we must help her even though her hands are not clean (our own are not either). We must not enter the war though we too may become involved in it in spite of trying to stay out.

But we must never forget that our object is peace when and as any chance of a peace that has any promise of being a real peace seems to offer we must do all we can to achieve it. We must be alert to take quick advantage of any such opening at any moment.

Meanwhile we should do what we can to get England openly and genuinely to commit herself to the sort of war aims and intended peace settlement that points to a peace of human welfare.

Especially we should ourselves state our own aims and make definite offers of what we are ready to contribute to help assure a world organized for peace. Specifically we should state now that we will internationalize the Panama Canal if other countries will cooperate to establish a complete system of internationalization of the open seas and of all waterways of an international character.

[1]Paul Van Zeeland (1893–1973) was Belgian prime minister (1935–1937) and delegate to various economic conferences (1922–1933). The Van Zeeland Report issued in January 1938 appealed to the WILPF and other peace groups because it offered a peaceful

means of settling the economic grievances of the "have-nots," the Germans and the Italians.

[2]Drew Pearson, a syndicated Washington Columnist, wrote the *Washington Merry Go Round*.

[3]Dorothy Detzer; see essay on pp. 131–133.

[4]Robert Allen was a prominent journalist.

[5]Bertrand Russell (1872–1970), the Britist philosopher, opposed World War I and was imprisoned in 1918 for his views. See his foresighted "Blueprint for An Enduring Peace," *The American Mercury* 52 (June 1941): 666–676.

[6]Robert Hutchins (1899–1977), the president of the University of Chicago, took an extreme isolationist stand in which he claimed that the United States would lose all its freedoms and moral principles if it entered the Second World War. See his "What Shall We Defend? We Are Losing Our Moral Principles," *Vital Speeches of the Day* 6 (1 July 1940): 546–549, and "The Path to War: We Are Drifting Into Suicide," *Vital Speeches of the Day* 8 (15 February 1941), 258–261.

[7]Jane Addams (1860–1935).

[8]Mohandas Gandhi (1869–1948) is esteemed for his doctrine of pacifist resistance to achieve political and social progress.

[9]*Pou sto* is probably an idiom from the Greek, "Here I stand."

[10]The Second Congress of the WILPF summoned by the International Committee of Women was held in May 1919 in Zurich. The Third Congress was held in July 1921 in Vienna.

[11]Reinhold Niebuhr (1892–1971), one of the most important American theologians of the twentieth century, had controversial views on Christian pacifism and greatly influenced the younger generation of intellectuals.

ELISABETH POTTS BROWN AND
JEAN R. SODERLUND

Sources on Quaker Women

The Haverford College Quaker Collection and the Swarthmore College Friends Historical Library contain remarkable sources for analysis. Both collections were begun by the Religious Society of Friends, whose members have been avid record makers and keepers since the seventeenth century. The Religious Society of Friends, founded in Commonwealth England by George Fox, was one of many religious dissenting groups of that time. Known as Quakers, they rejected many of the rituals, traditions, and doctrines of the Anglican and Presbyterian churches, including holy communion, baptism, the paid ministry, tithes, and hymn singing. The essential belief of Quakerism, that the Light, or God, is within every person, opened the way for women to participate fully in all religious functions from the very beginning. An early convert of Fox's was a woman and a minister, Elizabeth Hooton. Unlike in other religions, in which women were expected to remain silent, seventeenth-century Quaker women spread the Friends' message throughout the British Isles and to the Middle East and America, and challenged English authority with the same vigor as Quaker men.

Quaker Meeting Records

When George Fox and Margaret Fell developed an organizational structure of meetings in which lay people managed church business, they established separate meetings for women and men. The primary purpose of the business meetings was to oversee and guide all members of the meeting, and Friends believed they could do this most efficiently and with propriety if men and women supervised members of their own gender. Fox wrote that Friends should deal with women and men separately "for civility and modesty' sake."[1]

With a multilevel structure of meetings, Friends created an institutional framework for the Society without placing authority in the hands of one or a few men. Friends maintained discipline and made policy—and still do today—by reaching a "sense of the meeting," a kind of consensus in which participants agree that a decision is the will of God. If Friends cannot reach a sense of the meeting, the decision is postponed.

The Society established its multitiered system of meetings first in England and then throughout the world. On the primary level was the meeting for worship, in which men, women, and children met together for at least an hour once a week. At these meetings Friends waited in silence for God to speak through a participant, whether a woman or man. Members who had the gift for speaking in meeting were recognized as ministers, but the Society had no paid preachers. Quaker ministers needed no formal training or ordination. They had only to demonstrate, through their ministry, that they spoke the word of God. With no requirements save the spiritual, Quaker ministry has remained open to women throughout the Society's history.

The monthly meeting met once a month to conduct business concerning finances, property, and membership. Historically, a monthly meeting was composed of a few preparative meetings that were designed to "prepare" business for the meeting itself. Until the late nineteenth and early twentieth centuries women and men held separate monthly meetings to deliberate disciplinary decisions and discuss other business. The men's meeting considered a wider range of concerns than the women's meeting. The men had control of the meeting's property and made policy on such matters as slavery and holding public office in addition to taking care of business that the women also performed: disciplining members, providing certificates of removal for Friends moving to other places, supervising marriages, providing poor relief, and maintaining the Society's records. For example, when a couple wanted to marry, they announced their intention first to the women's monthly meeting and then to the men's meeting. The women appointed a committee to investigate whether the woman was "clear," that is, that she was unmarried and had not committed herself to another man. The men's meeting investigated the man in the same manner and both meetings had to give their approval before the marriage could proceed.

The next higher level is the quarterly meeting. Monthly meetings, which are geographically close together, appointed representatives to attend a quarterly meeting four times a year, which in turn appointed representatives to yearly meeting. The members of all the monthly meetings may gather at a yearly meeting, such as Philadelphia Yearly Meeting.

In America, women's meetings were organized at each level of the Society's hierarchy, in monthly, quarterly, and yearly meetings. Their special responsibilities were moral behavior of members, especially children; discipline of women and girls; care of the indigent and the ill; education of children; clearness for marriage; and care of the meeting house interior. Margaret Hope Bacon has said in *Mothers of Feminism:* "It was in the developing meetings for business that Quaker women learned to rely on their own strength and to develop their own talents together. In the nineteenth century, when observers began to note that many Quaker women took leadership in the women's rights movement, they credited the women's training in business meetings with providing the necessary experience."[2] Until the late eighteenth century, Quaker women's meetings were the only formal organizations in the United States run by women.

Minutes of the proceedings were recorded at each business session, at each level of the Society's structure. When Friends discuss and decide on a course of action, a minute of record is written with the exact wording agreed upon by the whole group. When a Quaker meeting wishes to communicate a formal message to other meetings, an epistle is sent to express the group's opinion on current theological, social, or political concerns.

Scholars can find materials of vital importance in Quaker records, which document the history of Quakerism, both in the United States and overseas, from the 1650s to the present. Indeed, the minutes of men's and women's meetings and registers of births, deaths, and marriages provide some of the earliest and most complete evidence about seventeenth- and eighteenth-century life. Though not all the records survive and some clerks were more thorough than others, the Society took pains to record the major events in the lives of its members.[3] As well as the customary vital statistics, Friends' meetings exchanged minutes when a member transferred to another meeting, sojourned for a short time, or visited several meetings as a traveling minister. All of these records track the individual and collective lives of Friends' and the events in their lives often reflected societal change. When American Friends split in the late 1820s, the branches founded parallel structures of church government and maintained their own records. Both sides called themselves the Religious Society of Friends, but they were commonly known as the Hicksite branch and the Orthodox branch.

Women and men served together on many meetings and committees such as those of ministers and elders, overseers, and school governance. Quakers in America always had a concern for basic literacy for their children. Many small short-lived meeting schools show up in records. Sometimes meeting schools were the predecessors of public schools, which continued to use meeting property until public facilities could be constructed.[4] Meetings of ministers and elders and committees of overseers labored with (discussed and struggled with) all of the members' spiritual and secular problems, their interactions with one another and with the larger society. Some of the discussion and the decisions reached were recorded in minutes available for study.

Some Quaker meeting records are in the hands of families of individuals who served as clerk or recording clerk of a meeting or of a committee. Some are still in the possession of the generating meeting. However, many yearly meetings have deposited their records and those of their constituent meetings in centralized locations for safekeeping; some are indexed and microfilmed. For example, the records of Philadelphia Yearly Meeting are on deposit at Friends Historical Library of Swarthmore College and the Quaker Collection at Haverford College. These records, which are sources for some of the social and demographic history of the mid-Atlantic region from the 1680s to the present, comprise about one thousand linear feet. Much of the material has been microfilmed and the depositories require researchers to use the films rather than the original materials. The terms by which Friends' meeting records are deposited generally preclude any lending and permit only limited copying. In order to improve access to records of Philadelphia Yearly Meeting and its over two hundred constituent meetings, the two colleges since 1986 have conducted a project to prepare coordinated inventories and a guide, which is to be published in 1989.

Committee and Institutional Records

Whan a Quaker has a social concern and wishes to take the step from faith to action, she or he tries to gather together Friends of like mind to form a committee. Some committees are overseen by a monthly, quarterly, or yearly meeting, and others are formed outside the purview of the Society of Friends and with non-Quakers. Over the more than three hundred years of the Society's existence, Friends have through group action expressed their concerns for education, the mentally ill, Native Americans, abolition of slavery, women's suffrage, and propagation of the faith. Records of the deliberations and actions of committees have been deposited in archives for use by researchers.

Some examples of committee work by women might be helpful. Quakers were very active in benevolent associations in the nineteenth century. The records of the Female Association for the Relief of Sick and Infirm Poor (1829–1973), the Hicksite organization that was formed after the separation and continued after reunification of the branches in 1955, are deposited at Swarthmore's Friends Historical Library. Deposited at the Quaker Collection at Haverford are the records of the Female Society of Philadelphia for the Relief and Employment of the Poor (1795–1978), which began before the separation, was continued by Orthodox Friends, and also remained in existence after 1955. Each of these collections consists of minutes, records of persons who were assisted with clothing and other necessities, treasurer's reports, subscribers' names, correspondence, and printed reports.

Often an institution, such as a school or hospital, was founded as the result of a committee's concern. For example, a group of New York and Philadelphia Orthodox Quakers established Haverford College in 1833 when it became obvious that there was a need for an institution of higher learning for male members of the Religious Society of Friends. Similarly, Bryn Mawr College for women was founded in 1885 by Orthodox Friends, and Swarthmore College in 1869 by Hicksite Friends as a coeducational college. Each college has an organized collection of archives, which are available for study.

Friends Hospital was established in 1813 as the Friends' Asylum for the Relief of Persons Deprived of the Use of Their Reason. The archives at the Quaker Collection include minutes of managers and superintendents, lists of contributors, blueprints, bills, maps, deeds, certificates, and pictures. The hospital ran an attendant's training school from the 1890s through the 1970s.

Papers of Families and Individuals

Quaker families and individuals have donated to various repositories the evidence of their thoughts and observations of activities over decades. These manuscript collections form another extremely valuable source of social history. All kinds of documents can be found: deeds, letters, journals and diaries, commonplace books, marriage certificates, maps, and wills. Whereas the meeting records provide continuous documentation of the functioning of a religious group in which women have played a vital role, the collections flesh out the lives of these women. Alongside the papers of well-known Quaker women such as Lucretia Mott (1793–1880) are the voluminous resources of unpublished papers of many lesser-known Friends. Quaker women such as Sarah Hill Dillwyn (1738–1826) and Sarah Garrett Scattergood (c. 1841–1889) left evidence of their roles in, and observations of, the Society, the meeting, and the family, as well as descriptions of their own process of self-awareness. Scholars have not yet mined much of this material.

For example, the papers of Mary Robinson Morton (1757–1829), a Rhode Island Quaker who moved to Philadelphia when she married in 1793, include personal correspondence, wills, printed almanacs with manuscript diary notations, and genealogical information. The correspondence reflects the social and cultural attitudes of the day, touching on the Hicksite controversy, the yellow fever epidemics of 1793 and 1798 in Philadelphia, as well as on the dreaded effects of smallpox.

The voluminous papers of a twentieth-century woman, Esther Biddle Rhoads (1896–1979) are at the Quaker Collection. She was a Philadelphia Quaker educator and social worker who was associated with Tokyo Friends Girls School (and the Japanese Royal family) as teacher, principal, and trustee from 1917 to 1977. She was also an American Friends Service Committee relief worker in Japan and Tunis. The collection of correspondence, committee reports, awards, scrapbooks, blueprints, photographs, and memorabilia records a lifetime of service.

The manuscript collections at Friends Historical Library include the papers of Margaretta Walton (1829–1904), an eminent Quaker minister of Chester and Bucks counties, Pennsylvania, who left an extensive series of journals, 1846–1902, describing her spiritual growth, travels in the ministry, and family life. In addition, there are copy and piece books from the 1840s as well as legal and business papers for herself and her husband, Jesse Pusey Walton (d. 1859). Among her correspondents was John Greenleaf Whittier.

In order to convince others of their experiential way of finding God and to defend themselves against verbal, physical, and legal abuse, Quaker women and men produced an unusually large number of tracts for a small sect. The Quaker Collection at Haverford College includes some two thousand pre-1700 tracts in which Friends speak in their own language about their convincement, their direct experiences with God, their right to be ministers (whether male or female), and their sufferings. Haverford has tracts written by forty-nine seventeenth-century women, including Margaret Fell's *Womens Speaking Justified, Proved and Allowed of by the Scriptures,* which was seminal in establishing the right of women to speak in the ministry.[5]

The "Dictionary of Quaker Biography" in typescript at the Quaker Collection and Friends House Library, London, includes outline biographies of some twenty-five thousand Quakers, covering the more than three hundred years of the existence worldwide of the Religious Society of Friends. Another extremely useful tool for identification of Friends (which has been only partially published) is the William Wade Hinshaw indexes to meeting records housed in Friends Historical Library.

Quaker Women and the Peace Movement

Women Friends have been active in benevolent and reform organizations since the late eighteenth century. Encouraged by the models of their mothers and empowered by their own experiences in meeting, Quaker women have created groups to deal with a wide range of social concerns. Among the most important to Friends has been their effort to secure global peace, to convince world leaders and their nations that conflicts can be resolved through nonviolent means. Quaker women and men have acted on the peace testimony of the Society of Friends by supporting and serving as conscientious objectors, providing war relief, lobbying governments for disarmament and reduced military expenditures, seeking to end hostilities among belligerents, establishing links between the people of unfriendly nations, and attempting to sway public opinion toward peaceful goals. They have also worked through peace organizations for civil rights, open housing, women's suffrage, and civil liberties.

The primary repository of records of the peace movement in the United States is the Swarthmore College Peace Collection. Among the women Friends whose papers can be found there are: Hannah J. Bailey (1839–1923), who was superintendent of the Department of Peace and Arbitration of the National Woman's Christian Temperance Union; Emily Greene Balch (1867–1961), one of the founders of the Women's International League for Peace and Freedom and a Nobel Peace Prize laureate who was involved in attempts to negotiate an end to World War I and made a fact-finding trip to Haiti in 1926; A. Ruth Fry (1872–1962), a British Quaker who was active in international relief projects, the Women's Peace Campaign, the War Resisters' International; Hannah Clothier Hull (1872–1958), a suffragist who was active in the Women's International League, the American Friends Service Committee, and Friends Peace Committee of Philadelphia Yearly Meeting; Dorothy Hutchinson (1905–1984), active in the Women's International League and a founder of the Women's Committee to Oppose Conscription.

A large proportion of the papers of Jane Addams (1860–1935) of Hull House in Chicago, a pioneering social worker, feminist, and pacifist who was not a Friend herself but whose father was a Hicksite Quaker, are in the Peace Collection and others are held by the University of Illinois. *The Jane Addams Papers,* a comprehensive microfilm edition compiled by Mary Lynn McCree Bryan and others, contains correspondence of Quaker women and is available from University Microfilms International. Friends Historical Library of Swarthmore College holds a significant collection of the papers of Lucretia Mott, who was involved in William Lloyd Garrison's New England Non-Resistance Society and the Pennsylvania Peace Society along with her many other activities for women's rights and the abolition of slavery.

Other sources documenting the work of Quaker women in the peace movement are the records of Quaker organizations. The Peace Collection holds the records of Friends Peace Committee of Philadelphia Yearly Meeting jointly with Friends Historical Library. The Friends Peace Committee records date from 1891 and include the papers of the separate committees created by the Hicksite and Orthodox branches; the peace committees merged in 1933, before reunification of the two branches. For the American Friends Service Committee, the Peace Collection has records of the Peace Education Division, National Action/Research on the Military-Industrial Complex (NARMIC), and the Central America Working Group. The primary repository of American Friends Service Committee records is the Service Committee's archives in Philadelphia. Also available in the Swarthmore College Peace Collection are records of the Friends Committee on National Legislation (1940 to date), the Quaker lobbying group headquartered in Washington, D. C., the Peace Association of Friends in America (records 1868–1943), organized for peace education in 1867 by Orthodox Friends in New York, Baltimore, North Carolina, Ohio, Indiana, Western, and Iowa yearly meetings; and A Quaker Action Group (records 1966–1971), founded in Philadelphia to "apply nonviolent direct action as a witness against the war in Vietnam."

Quaker women have also participated in peace groups with no official or unofficial ties to the Religious Society of Friends. The Peace Collection has records of many of these organizations, including such nineteenth-century groups as the American Peace Society (founded in 1828), an association of several regional peace societies that promoted international peace congresses and use of arbitration; the Universal Peace Union (founded in 1866), which supported unilateral disarmament, abolition of capital punishment, women's suffrage, and justice for Native Americans; the Pennsylvania Peace Society (founded in 1866), closely related to the Universal Peace Union; and the Wisbech (England) Local Peace Association, of which British Friend Priscilla H. Peckover was a founder.

In the twentieth century women Friends have participated in a large number of peace groups, those including both men and women and those founded by women alone. Among these organizations is the Fellowship of Reconciliation, which was established in 1914 by Christian pacifists but now attracts members of many religions. The fellowship is an international group of men and women that has been involved in efforts for civil rights, economic justice, and civil liberties as well as for disarmament and nonviolent conflict resolution.

The Women's International League for Peace and Freedom was founded in 1915 by Jane Addams, Carrie Chapmen Catt, Emily Greene Balch, and others, and since its earliest years has consistently had Quakers among its leaders. Women's International League members attempted to negotiate an end to World War I and since then have tried to affect government policy by lobbying decision makers and influencing public opinion. The U.S. section of the league has its headquarters in Philadelphia and is part of WILPF International, which is headquartered in Geneva. The Swarthmore College Peace Collection is the official repository for the U.S. section, of which most of the pre-1960 records are on microfilm and available from Scholarly Resources, Inc. The Peace Collection also has some WILPF International records, but the main body of these records is housed at the University of Colorado; they are also on microfilm, available from University Microfilms International. The Bentley Historical Library, Minnesota Historical Society, Schlesinger Library, and Sophia Smith Collection have records of individual state branches or other small collections of Women's International League records. The Peoples Mandate, which started in 1935 as a project of the WILPF International executive committee, attempted to collect fifty million signatures against war from the citizens of fifty countries. Records of the U.S. section of the Peoples Mandate are in the Swarthmore College Peace Collection.

Quaker women have also participated in the War Resisters League, which was established in 1923 as an alternative to women's peace groups such as the Women's International League and groups with a religious basis such as the Fellowship of Reconciliation. The War Resisters League pledged to "enroll all persons who were absolutely opposed to war, irrespective of sex or religion." Another peace organization in which women Friends were involved was the

National Council for Prevention of War, founded in 1921 as a clearinghouse for the peace movement. The National Council, of which only organizations could be members, coordinated speaking tours and lobbying efforts, and issued publications. Mildred Scott Olmsted, a Quaker and Women's International League leader, was director of the Women's Committee to Oppose Conscription, which worked in the years 1942 to 1950 to defeat a proposal to draft nurses and then opposed peacetime conscription after World War II. Radical pacifists founded the Committee for Nonviolent Action in 1957 to oppose nuclear weapons with nonviolent direct action. They sponsored peace walks, vigils, demonstrations at the Atomic Energy Commission, and voyages into nuclear testing zones to promote public awareness of the nuclear threat and to attempt to bring an end to nuclear tests. In 1961, a group of Washington, D.C., women began Women Strike for Peace as a one-day effort against nuclear weapons. The loosely knit organization spread throughout the country and is credited with developing considerable support for the partial Test Ban Treaty of 1963. The group also opposed the Vietnam War at an early date. The records of all of these organizations are in the Swarthmore College Peace Collection.

Additional Information

Chmielewski, Wendy E., ed. *Guide to Sources on Women in the Swarthmore College Peace Collection.* Swarthmore, Pa.: Swarthmore College, 1988.

Green, Marguerite, ed. *Peace Archives: A Guide to Library Collections.* Berkeley, Calif.: World Without War Council, 1986.

Guide to the Manuscript Collections of Friends Historical Library of Swarthmore College. Swarthmore, Pa.: Swarthmore College, 1982.

Guide to the Records of Philadelphia Yearly Meeting of the Religious Society of Friends at the Quaker Collection and Friends Historical Library. Philadelphia, Pa.: Records Committee of Philadelphia Yearly Meeting, Haverford College and Swarthmore College, 1989.

Guide to the Swarthmore College Peace Collection. 2d ed. Swarthmore, Pa.: Swarthmore College, 1981.

Hinding, Andrea, ed. *Woman's History Sources: A Guide to Archives and Manuscript Collections in the United States.* 2 vols. New York: Bowker, 1979.

Vaux, Trina, ed. *Guide to Women's History Resources in the Delaware Valley Area.* Philadelphia, Pa.: University of Pennsylvania Press, 1983.

Women, War, and Peace: A Selected Bibliography and Filmography. New Brunswick, N.J.: Institute for Research on Women, Rutgers University, 1986.

NOTES

1. Fox's letter of 30 Jan. 1675, quoted in William C. Braithwaite, *The Second Period of Quakerism,* ed. Henry J. Cadbury, 2d ed. (Cambridge: Cambridge University Press, 1961), 274.

2. Margaret Hope Bacon, *Mothers of Feminism: The Story of Quaker Women in America* (San Francisco: Harper & Row, 1986), 42.

3. There are some restrictions on use of family names in some of these records. For example, Jack D. Marietta was restricted to using initials when referring to people in his study of disciplinary records, *The Reformation of American Quakerism, 1748–1783* (Philadelphia: University of Pennsylvania Press, 1984).

4. For example: Friends School at Crosswicks, Crosswicks, Burlington County, New Jersey.

5. Margaret Fell, *Womens Speaking Justified, Proved and Allowed of by the Scriptures* (London: N.p., 1666).

Bibliography

Printed Primary Sources

Burrough, Edward. *An Alarm to all Flesh; with an Invitation to the True Seeker, forthwith to Fly for his Life (clearly) out of the Shortliv'd Babylon, into the Life, etc.* London: For Robert Wilson, 1660.

Burrough, Edward. *A Warning from the Lord to the Inhabitants of Underbarrow, and so to all the Inhabitants in England.* London: For Giles Calvert, 1654.

Camm, John, and John Audland. *The Memory of the Righteous Revived.* London: Andrew Sowle, 1689.

Cotton, Priscilla, and Mary Cole. *To the Priests and People of England, We Discharge our Consciences, and Give Them Warning.* London: For Giles Calvert, 1655.

Eccles, Solomon. *In the Yeare 59 in the Fourth Month.* London: Printed for M. W., 1659.

Evans, Katherine, and Sarah Cheevers. *This is a Short Relation of Some of the Cruel Sufferings (for the Truths Sake) of Katherine Evans & Sarah Chevers, in the Inquisition in the Isle of Malta.* London: For Robert Wilson, 1662.

Farmer, Ralph. *Sathan Enthron'd in his Chair of Pestilence, or Quakerism in its Exaltation.* London: For Edward Thomas, 1657.

Farnworth, Richard. *A Woman Forbidden to Speak in the Church.* London: For Giles Calvert, 1654.

Fell, Margaret. *Womens Speaking Justified, Proved and Allowed of by the Scriptures.* London: N.p., 1666.

Hendricks, Elizabeth. *An Epistle to Friends in England, To be Read in their Assemblies in the Fear of the Lord.* London: N.p., 1672.

Howgill, Francis. *A Testimony Concerning the Life, Death, Trials, Travels and Labours of Edward Burroughs, that Worthy Prophet of the Lord who dyed a prisoner for the Testimony of Jesus, and the Word of God, in the City of London, the 14th of the 12th Month, 1662.* London: William Warwick, 1662.

Howgill, Mary. *A Remarkable Letter of Mary Howgill to Oliver Cromwell, called Protector.* London: N.p., 1657.

Hubberthorn, Richard. *A Collection of the Several Books and Writings of that Faithful Servant of God Richard Hubberthorn.* London: Printed for William Warwick, 1663.

Keith, George. *The Woman Preacher of Samaria.* London: N.p., 1674.

Killam, Margaret. *A Warning from the Lord to the Teachers and the People of Plimouth.* London: For Giles Calvert, 1656.

Bibliography

Nayler, James. *An Answer to 28 Queries Sent Out by Francis Harris to those People He Calls Quakers*. London: For Giles Calvert, 1655.

———. *A Discovery of the Man of Sin*. London: For Giles Calvert, 1655.

The Saints Testimony Finishing through Sufferings: or, The Proceedings of the Court against the Servants of Jesus . . . held in Banbury. London: For Giles Calvert, 1655.

Taylor, Thomas, and Elizabeth Hooton. *To the King and Both Houses of Parliament*. N.p.: 1670.

White, Dorothy. *An Epistle of Love, and of Consolation unto Israel*. London: Printed for Robert Wilson, 1661.

Secondary Sources

Addams, Jane, Emily Greene Balch, and Alice Hamilton. *Women at The Hague: The International Congress of Women and its Results*. 1915; New York: Garland, 1972.

Alonso, Harriet Hyman. "Putting Pacifism into Practice: Women Peace Activists and the Geneva Disarmament Conference of 1932." Paper read at Seventh Berkshire Conference on the History of Women, Wellesley College, 21 June 1987.

Bacon, Margaret Hope. *As the Way Opens: The Story of Quaker Women in America*. Richmond, Ind.: Friends United Press, 1980.

———. *Mothers of Feminism: The Story of Quaker Women in America*. San Francisco: Harper & Row, 1986.

———. *Valiant Friend: The Life of Lucretia Mott*. New York: Walker, 1980.

Balch, Emily Greene, ed. *Occupied Haiti*. New York: The Writer's Publishing Company, 1927.

Baltzell, Digby. *Puritan Boston and Quaker Philadelphia: Two Protestant Ethics and the Spirit of Class Authority*. New York: Free Press, 1979.

Bandel, Betty. "English Chroniclers' Attitude toward Women." *The Journal of the History of Ideas* 16 (1955): 113–118.

Barbour, Hugh. *The Quakers in Puritan England*. New Haven: Yale University Press, 1964.

———. and Arthur O. Roberts, eds. *Early Quaker Writings, 1650–1700*. Grand Rapids: Eerdmans, 1973.

Beasley, Maurine Hoffman, ed. *The White House Press Conferences of Eleanor Roosevelt*. New York and London: Garland, 1983.

Bede. *A History of the English Church and People*. Trans. L. Sherley-Price. Rev. ed. London: Dent, 1968.

Berkin, Carol Ruth, and Mary Beth Norton, eds. *Women of America: A History*. Boston: Houghton Mifflin, 1979.

Besse, Joseph. *A Collection of the Sufferings of the People Called Quakers*. London: L. Hinde, 1753.

Boeckel, Florence Brewer. "Women in International Affairs." *Annals of the American Academy of Political and Social Science* 143 (May 1929): 230–248.

Bibliography

Bouwsma, William. *John Calvin: A Sixteenth-Century Portrait.* New York: Oxford, 1988.

Bowden, James. *The History of the Society of Friends in America.* 2 vols. London: C. Gilpin, 1850.

Bradley, A. Day. "Progressive Friends in Michigan and New York." *Quaker History* 52 (1963): 95–103.

Brailsford, Mabel Richmond. *Quaker Women, 1650–1690.* London: Duckworth, 1915.

Braithwaite, William C. *The Beginnings of Quakerism.* Revised by Henry J. Cadbury. 2d ed. Cambridge: Cambridge University Press, 1955.

———. *The Second Period of Quakerism.* Edited by Henry J. Cadbury. 2d ed. Cambridge: Cambridge University Press, 1961.

Bridenthal, Renate, and Claudia Koonz, eds. *Becoming Visible: Women in European History.* Boston: Houghton Mifflin, 1977.

———; Claudia Koonz; and Susan Stuard, eds. *Becoming Visible.* Boston: Houghton Mifflin, 1987.

Brinton, Howard H. *Friends for 300 Years: The History and Beliefs of the Society of Friends since George Fox Started the Quaker Movement.* New York: Harper, 1952.

———. *The Peace Testimony of the Society of Friends.* Philadelphia: American Friends Service Committee, 1958.

Brock, Peter. *Pioneers of the Peaceable Kingdom.* Princeton: Princeton University Press, 1968.

Bronner, Edwin B. "An Early Example of Political Action by Women." *Bulletin of the Friends Historical Association* 43 (1954): 29–32.

Brown, Dorothy M. *Setting a Course: American Women in the 1920s.* Boston: Twayne, 1987.

Bussey, Gertrude, and Margaret Tims. *Pioneers for Peace: Women's International League for Peace and Freedom, 1915–1965.* London: WILPF British Section, 1980.

Bynum, Caroline. *Jesus as Mother: Studies in the Spirituality of the High Middle Ages.* Berkeley: University of California Press, 1982.

Carroll, Kenneth L. "Early Quakers and 'Going Naked as Sign'." *Quaker History* 67:2 (Autumn 1978): 69–87.

———. "Elizabeth Harris, the Founder of American Quakerism." *Quaker History* 57:2 (Autumn 1968): 96–98.

Chatfield, Charles. "World War I and the Liberal Pacifist in the United States." *American Historical Review* 75 (1970): 1920–1937.

Chmielewski, Wendy E., ed. *Guide to Sources on Women in the Swarthmore College Peace Collection.* Swarthmore, Pa.: Swarthmore College, 1988.

Colie, Rosali. *Paradoxia Epidemica: The Renaissance Tradition of Paradox.* Princeton: Princeton University Press, 1966.

Colledge, E., and J. Walsh, eds. *A Book of Showings to the Anchoress Julian of Norwich.* Toronto: PIMS, 1978.

Colman, Lucy N. *Reminiscences.* Buffalo, N.Y.: H.L. Green, 1891.

Bibliography

Comly, John, and Isaac Comly, eds. *Friends' Miscellany.* 12 vols. Philadelphia: William Sharpless, 1831–1839.

Cott, Nancy F. *The Grounding of Modern Feminism.* New Haven: Yale University Press, 1987.

———and Elizabeth H. Pleck, eds. *A Heritage of Her Own: Toward a New Social History of American Women.* New York: Simon and Schuster, 1979.

Curti, Merle. *Peace or War: The American Struggle, 1636–1936.* New York: W.W. Norton, 1936.

Davidson, Carlisle G. "A Profile of Hicksite Quakerism in Michigan, 1830–1860." *Quaker History* 59 (1970): 106–112.

Davis, Natalie Z. *Society and Culture in Early Modern France.* Stanford: Stanford University Press, 1975.

Delamaine, A. and T. Terry, eds. *A Volume of Spiritual Epistles . . . by John Reeve and Lodowicke Muggleton.* N.p., 1755.

Detzer, Dorothy. *Appointment on the Hill.* New York: Henry Holt, 1940.

DiStefano, Judy Mann. "The Concept of the Family in Colonial America: The Pembertons of Philadelphia." Ph.D. diss., Ohio State University, 1970.

Divine, Robert A. *The Illusion of Neutrality.* Chicago: University of Chicago Press, 1962.

Drinker, Sophie Lewis Hutchinson. *Pennsylvania's Honored Mistress: Unanswered Questions in the Life of Hannah Callowhill Penn.* Paper read before the Welcome Society, January 1959.

Dunn, Richard S., and Mary Maples Dunn, eds. *The World of William Penn.* Philadelphia: University of Pennsylvania Press, 1986.

Early, Frances H. "The Historic Roots of the Women's Peace Movement in North America." *Canadian Woman Studies* 7 (Winter 1986): 43–48.

———. "An Interview with Mildred Scott Olmsted: Foremother of the Women's International League for Peace and Freedom." *Atlantis* 12 (Fall 1986): 142–150.

Eisler, Riane. *The Chalice and the Blade: Our History, Our Future.* Cambridge, Mass.: Harper, 1987.

Elias, Norbert. *The History of Manners.* Vol. 1, *The Civilizing Process,* Trans. Edmund Jephcott. New York: Pantheon Books, 1982.

Fabrizio, Linda. "The Challenge Accepted: The European Woman of WILPF Against Fascism." Paper read at Seventh Berkshire Conference on the History of Women, Wellesley College, 20 June 1987.

Faith and Practice. Worcester, Mass.: New England Yearly Meeting of Friends, 1985.

"Feminist Friends: Agrarian Quakers and the Emergence of Woman's Rights in America." *Feminist Studies* 12:1 (Spring 1986): 27–49.

Flexner, Eleanor. *Century of Struggle: The Woman's Rights Movement in the United States.* Cambridge: Harvard University Press, 1959.

Foster-Hayes, Carrie. "The Women and the Warriors: Dorothy Detzer and the WILPF." Ph.D. diss., University of Denver, 1984.

Bibliography

Fox, George. *A Collection of Many Select and Christian Epistles, Letters, and Testimonies*. London: T. Sowle, 1698.

———. *Journal*. 2 vols. Ed. Norman Penney. Cambridge: Cambridge University Press, 1911.

———. *Journal*. Rev. ed. by John L. Nickalls. London: Religious Society of Friends, 1975.

———. *The Works of George Fox*. 8 vols. Philadelphia: M.T.C. Gould, 1831.

———. *Book of Miracles*. Ed. Henry J. Cadbury. New York: Octagon Books, 1973.

Friedman, Jean E., and William G. Shade, eds. *Our American Sisters: Women in American Life and Thought*. 3d ed. Lexington, Mass.: D.C. Heath, 1982.

Frost, J. William. *The Quaker Family in Colonial America: A Portrait of the Society of Friends*. New York: St. Martin's Press, 1973.

———and John M. Moore, eds. *Seeking the Light: Essays in Quaker History in Honor of Edwin B. Bronner*. Wallingford, Pa.: Pendle Hill Publications; Haverford, Pa.: Friends Historical Association, 1986.

Gadt, Jeanette. "Women and Protestant Culture: The Quaker Dissent from Puritanism." Ph.D. diss. U.C.L.A., 1974.

Green, Marguerite, ed. *Peace Archives: A Guide to Library Collections of the Papers of American Peace Organizations and of Leaders in the Public Effort for Peace*. Berkeley, Calif.: World Without War Council, 1986.

Guide to the Manuscript Collections of Friends Historical Library of Swarthmore College. Swarthmore, Pa.: Swarthmore College, 1982.

Guide to the Records of Philadelphia Yearly Meeting of the Religious Society of Friends at the Quaker Collection and Friends Historical Library. Philadelphia: Records Committee of Philadelphia Yearly Meeting, Haverford College and Swarthmore College, 1989.

Guide to the Swarthmore College Peace Collection. 2d ed. Swarthmore, Pa.: Swarthmore College, 1982.

Gummere, Amelia Mott. *The Quaker: a Study in Costume*. New York: B. Blom, 1968.

Hartman, Mary, and Lois Banner, eds. *Clio's Consciousness Raised: New Perspectives on the History of Women*. New York: Harper & Row, 1974.

Heiss, Willard, ed. *Quaker Biographical Sketches of Ministers and Elders and Other Concerned Members of the Yearly Meeting of Philadelphia 1682–1800*. Indianapolis: published for the author, 1972.

Hewitt, Nancy A. "Amy Kirby Post." *The University of Rochester Library Bulletin* 37 (1984): 5–21.

———. *Women's Activism and Social Change: Rochester, New York, 1822–1872*. Ithaca, N.Y.: Cornell University Press, 1984.

Hill, Christopher. *The World Turned Upside Down: Radical Ideas during the English Revolution*. New York: Viking, 1972.

Hinding, Andrea, ed. *Women's History Sources: A Guide to Archives and Manuscript Collections in the United States*. 2 vols. New York: Bowker, 1979.

Hodgkin, Lucy V. *A Quaker Saint of Cornwall: Loveday Hambly and her Guests.* London: Longmans Green, 1927.

Hutchins, Robert. "The Path to War: We are Drifting into Suicide." *Vital Speeches of the Day* 8 (February 15, 1941): 258–261.

——. "What shall we Defend? We are losing our Moral Principles." *Vital Speeches of the Day* 6 (July 1, 1940): 546–549.

Ingle, H. Larry. *Quakers in Conflict: The Hicksite Reformation.* Knoxville: University of Tennessee Press, 1986.

James, Edward T.; Janet Wilson James; and Paul S. Boyer, eds. *Notable American Women, 1607–1950: A Biographical Dictionary.* 3 vols. Cambridge: Belknap Press of Harvard University Press, 1971.

James, Janet Wilson, ed. *Women in American Religion.* Philadelphia: University of Pennsylvania Press, 1980.

James, Sydney. *A People among Peoples: Quaker Benevolence in Eighteenth-Century America.* Cambridge: Harvard University Press, 1963.

Jelinek, Estelle, ed. *Women's Autobiography: Essays in Criticism.* Bloomington: University of Indiana Press, 1980.

Jensen, Joan M. *Loosening the Bonds: Mid-Atlantic Farm Women, 1750–1850.* New Haven: Yale University Press, 1986.

Jones, Rufus M. *The Later Periods of Quakerism.* 2 vols. 1921; Westport, Conn.: Greenwood Press, 1970.

——. *Mysticism and Democracy in the English Commonwealth.* Cambridge: Harvard University Press, 1932.

——. *The Quakers in the American Colonies.* London: Macmillan, 1911.

——. *Studies in Mystical Religion.* London: Macmillan, 1909.

Jorns, Auguste. *The Quakers as Pioneers in Social Work.* Trans. Thomas Kite Brown, Jr. New York: Macmillan, 1931.

Kelly, Joan. *Women, History and Theory.* Chicago: University of Chicago Press, 1984.

Klassen, John. "Women and Religious Reform in Late Medieval Bohemia." *Renaissance and Reformation* 5:4 (1981): 203–221.

Knox, Ronald. *Enthusiasm: A Chapter in the History of Religion, with Special Reference to the XVII and XVIII Centuries.* Oxford: Oxford University Press, 1950.

Koehler, Lyle. *A Search for Power: The "Weaker Sex" in Seventeenth-Century New England.* Urbana: University of Illinois Press, 1980.

Kramer, H., and J. Sprenger. *Malleus Maleficarum.* Trans. Montague Summers. London: Rodker, 1928.

Kunze, Bonnelyn Young. "The Family, Social and Religious Life of Margaret Fell." Ph.D. diss., University of Rochester, 1986.

Lemons, J. Stanley. *The Woman Citizen: Social Feminism in the 1920s.* Urbana: University of Illinois Press, 1973.

Lerner, Gerda. *The Creation of Patriarchy.* New York: Oxford University Press, 1986.

Levy, Barry. *Quakers and the American Family: British Settlement in the Delaware Valley.* New York: Oxford University Press, 1988.

Bibliography

Locker-Lampson, Sophie Felicité, ed. *A Quaker Post-bag*. London: Longmans Green, 1910.

Lovejoy, David S. *Religious Enthusiasm in the New World.: Heresy to Revolution*. Cambridge: Harvard University Press, 1985.

Luther, Martin. *Werke. Kritische Gesamtausgabe*. Weimer: H. Bohlaus Nachfolger, 1883.

Maclean, Ian. *The Renaissance Notion of Woman: A Study in the Fortunes of Scholasticism and Medical Science in European Intellectual Life*. Cambridge: Cambridge University Press, 1980.

————. *Woman Triumphant: Feminism in French Literature 1610–1652*. Oxford: Oxford University Press, 1977.

Manners, Emily. *Elizabeth Hooton: First Quaker Woman Preacher (1600–1672)*. London: Headley Bros., 1911.

Marchand, C. Roland. *The American Peace Movement and Social Reform, 1898–1918*. Princeton: Princeton University Press,.1972.

Marietta, Jack D. *The Reformation of American Quakerism, 1748–1783*. Philadelphia: University of Pennsylvania Press, 1984.

Moore, John M., ed. *Friends in the Delaware Valley: Philadelphia Yearly Meeting, 1681–1981*. Haverford, Pa.: Friends Historical Association, 1981.

Nuttall, Geoffrey. *The Holy Spirit in Puritan Faith and Experience*. Oxford: Basil Blackwell, 1946.

————., comp. *Early Quaker Letters from the Swarthmore Mss. to 1660*. London: The Library, Friends House, 1952.

"On Registering Women." *Independent Woman* 26:5 (1919), 145–146.

Pagels, Elaine. *Adam, Eve and the Serpent in Genesis 1–3*. Claremont, Calif.: Institute for Antiquity and Christianity, 1987.

————. *Gnostic Gospels: A New Account of the Origins of Christianity*. New York: Random, 1979.

Paul, Alice. "Conversations with Alice Paul: Woman Suffrage and the Equal Rights Amendment: An Interview Conducted by Amelia Fry in 1972." Berkeley: The Bancroft Library, University of California, 1976.

Penney, Norman, ed. "*The First Publishers of Truth*" *Being Early Records . . . of the Introduction of Quakerism into the Counties of England and Wales*. London: Headley Bros., 1907.

Quaker Women's Group. *Bringing the Invisible into the Light: Some Quaker Feminists Speak of Their Experience*. Swarthmore Lecture 1986. London: Quaker Home Service, 1986.

Randall, Mercedes. *Improper Bostonian: Emily Greene Balch*. New York: Twayne, 1964.

Ross, Isabel. *Margaret Fell: Mother of Quakerism*. London: Longmans Green, 1949; York, England: William Sessions, Ebor Press, 1984.

Russell, Bertrand. "Blueprint for an Enduring Peace." *The American Mercury* 52 (June 1941): 666–676.

Scharf, Lois, and Joan M. Jensen, eds. *Decades of Discontent: The Women's Movement, 1920–1940*. Westport, Conn.: Greenwood Press, 1983.

Bibliography

Scull, G. D. *Dorothea Scott, Otherwise Gotherson & Hogben, of Egerton House, Kent, 1611–1680*. Oxford: Parker & Co., 1883.

Sicherman, Barbara. *Alice Hamilton: A Life in Letters*. Cambridge: Harvard University Press, 1984.

———, and Carol Hurd Green, eds. *Notable American Women: The Modern Period: A Biographical Dictionary*. Cambridge: Belknap Press of Harvard University Press, 1980.

Smith-Rosenberg, Carroll. *Disorderly Conduct: Visions of Gender in Victorian America*. New York: Knopf, 1985.

Smith, Nigel. "The Interior Word: Aspects of the Use of Language and Rhetoric in Radical Puritan and Sectarian Literature, c.1640–c.1660." D. Phil. diss., Oxford, 1985.

Soderlund, Jean R. "Women's Authority in Pennsylvania and New Jersey Quaker Meetings, 1680–1760." *William and Mary Quarterly* 3:44 (1987): 722–749.

Solomon, Barbara Miller. *Ancestors and Immigrants: A Changing New England Tradition*. Cambridge: Harvard University Press, 1956.

Speizman, Milton D., and Jane C. Kronick, "A Seventeenth-Century Quaker Women's Declaration." SIGNS 1:1 (1975): 231–245.

Stanton, Elizabeth Cady, et al. *History of Woman Suffrage*. New York: Fowler and Wells, 1881.

Stone, Lawrence. *The Family, Sex and Marriage in England, 1500–1800*. New York: Harper & Row, 1977.

Stoneburner, Carol, and John Stoneburner, eds. *The Influence of Quaker Women on American History: Biographical Studies*. Lewiston, N.Y.: Edwin Mellen, 1986.

Thomas, Keith. "Women in the Civil War Sects." *Past and Present* 13 (1958): 42–62.

Tolles, Frederick B. "Partners for Peace: William I. Hull and Hannah Clothier Hull." *Swarthmore Alumni Issue* (December 1958): 3, 44–45.

Trueblood, D. Elton. "The Quaker Way." *Atlantic Monthly* 166 (1940): 740–746.

Van Voris, Jacqueline. *College: A Smith Mosaic*. West Springfield, Mass.: Smith College, 1975.

Vann, Richard T. *The Social Development of English Quakerism, 1655–1755*. Cambridge: Harvard University Press, 1969.

Vaux, Trina, ed. *Guide to Women's History Resources in the Delaware Valley Area*. Philadelphia: University of Pennsylvania Press, 1983.

Vipont, Elfrida. *The Story of Quakerism, 1652–1952*. London: Bannisdale, 1954.

Wemple, Suzanne. *Women in Frankish Society: Marriage and the Cloister, 500 to 900*. Philadelphia: University of Pennsylvania Press, 1981.

Wister, Sarah. *The Journal and Occasional Writings of Sarah Wister*. Ed. Kathryn Zabelle Derounian. Rutherford: Fairleigh Dickinson University Press, 1987.

Bibliography

Women, War, and Peace: A Selected Bibliography and Filmography. New Brunswick, N.J.: Institute for Research on Women, Rutgers University, 1986.

Worrall, Arthur J. *Quakers in the Colonial Northeast.* Hanover, N.H.: University Press of New England, 1980.

Wight, Thomas, and John Rutty. *A History of the Rise and Progress of the People Called Quakers in Ireland.* Dublin: I. Jackson, 1751.

Wright, Luella. *The Literary Life of the Early Friends, 1650–1725.* New York: Columbia University Press, 1932.

Zuckerman, Michael, ed. *Friends and Neighbors: Group Life in America's First Plural Society.* Philadelphia: Temple University Press, 1982.

Index

Index

conversion, 31, 46; female, 51, 56; male, 52
convinced Quaker, 20
Cotton, Priscilla, 49
Cromwell, Oliver, 41, 45
Crouch, Mildred, 51
culture, mnemonic, 38
Curtis, Barbara, viii
Czechoslovakia, 136

Davies, Eleanor, 47
Deborah, 40, 49
Debs, Eugene, 126
DeGarmo, Rhoda, 112, 119
demographic history, 160
Detzer, Dorothy, 131, 132–133, 135, 136–137, 140, 141, 149–150
devil, the, 10, 11, 28, 38
diaries, 162
"Dictionary of Quaker Biography," 163
Dillwyn, Sarah Hill, 162
disarmament, 133, 164–165
discipline, 105
disownment, 101
Divine Love, 5, 37
Divine Revelation, 13
dogma, 12
Dollar, Margaret, 143
domesticity, 82
Downer, Ann, 55
Drinker, Sophie, 76
Duchene, Gabrielle, 137
Dudley, Mary, 95–96
Dunn, Mary Maples, 17
Dunn, Richard, 80
Dyer, Mary, 73, 81

Early, Frances, viii, 143
Eccles, Solomon, 51
Eden, 56
Edkins, Carol, 79
education, 17, 19, 128, 159
Edwin, King of Northumbria, 5

egalitarianism, 40
elders, 100, 101, 104
Elgar, Sarah, 96
elitism, 20–21
Elwood's journal, 111
emancipation, 35
Emergency Peace Federation, 125
emotion, 36
England, 4, 10, 13, 21, 31, 41, 44, 45, 46, 51, 74, 81, 153–155, 157, 158, 164, 165; north of, 45; seventeenth century, 72; south of, 45, 46. *See also* Great Britain
Enlightenment, 40, 94
enthusiasm, 35, 40
equality, 6, 100, 127–128
equal rights, 112, 114
Equal Rights Amendment, 131
Esther, 40
Ethiopia, 135
Europe, 43, 96, 128, 135, 148
Evans, Katherine, 38
Eve, 9
existentialism, 41

Fabrizio, Linda, 137, 143
family, 13, 18, 44, 57, 72, 80, 83, 162; Quaker, 19, 20, 47, 51, 72, 80, 83; rural, 83
Farmington, New York, 103, 112
Farnsworth, Richard, 48
fascism, 123, 137
fathers, 19; fathers in Israel, 56
Fell, Margaret, vii, 12, 15, 25, 35, 42, 43, 45, 52, 54, 55, 64, 66, 72, 73, 76, 157, 163; daughters of, 15, 25, 73
Fell, Mary, 25, 33
Fell, Sarah, 25, 73
Fellowship of Reconciliation, 125, 126, 166
Female Association for the Relief of the Sick and Infirm Poor, 161

husbands, 8, 10
Hussites, 8
Hutchins, Robert, 152, 156
Hutchinson, Anne, 35
Hutchinson, Dorothy, 164
idolatry, 44
imagery, 46, 48

Imlay, Maria, 99
imperialism, 151
Independent Woman, 141
India, 154
Indiana, 97, 99, 103, 112, 165
Ingle, H. Larry, 93, 96
intemperance, 116
international affairs, 129
International Alliance of Women for
    Suffrage and Equal Citizenship,
    129
International Association of Univer-
    sity Women, 129
internationalization of the seas, 155
inward guide, 87
Iowa, 165
Ireland, 38, 95, 96
Italy, 136

Jamaica, 32
Japan, 21, 135, 136, 138, 162
Jensen, Joan M., 79, 82–83
Jeremiah, 38, 44
Jericho, New York, 97
Jerusalem, 51
Jesus Christ, 5, 15, 25, 26, 28, 48,
    51, 52, 73, 100, 126. *See also* God
Jews, 47, 137, 154
Johnson, Phebe, 99
Jonah, 44
Jones, Ann, 99
Jones, George, 99
Jones, Norris, 96
Jones, Rebecca, 96
Jones, Rufus M., 93, 95
Jost, Ursula, 8

Julian of Norwich, 5
justice, 117

Keith, George, 49
Kelley, Abby, 101
Kellogg-Briand Peace Pact, 133, 151
Kelly, Joan, 8, 94
Killam, Joan, 64
Killam, Margaret, 37, 46, 47, 64
Kirby, Amy, 99. *See also* Post, Amy
    Kirby
Kirby, Mary, 86, 87, 102, 108, 109
Knox, Ronald, 34
Koehler, Lyle, 93
Kronick, Jane C., 25
Kunze, Bonnelyn Young, 73, 76

Ladd, Hannah, 87
Ladd, John, 87
Lamphere, Louise, 77
Lancashire, England, 45, 64
Lancashire Meeting of Women
    Friends, 15, 25
Lancaster, James, 32
lawyers, 8
leadership, Quaker, 132, 142
League of Nations, 135
Leavens, Elizabeth, 49
Levellers, 10
Levy, Barry, 73, 79, 80, 81, 83
liberalism, 131
licentiousness, 116
Light, 14, 34, 37, 39, 99, 157
literacy, 8, 28
lobbying, 166
Lollards, 8
London, England, 16, 46, 47, 64,
    163
London Yearly Meeting, 16, 103
Long Island, New York, 97
Long Island Monthly Meeting, 100
Lord, John, 87
Lovejoy, David, 35
Lower, Abraham, 98